GREAT AMERICAN

FOR
JAMES BEARD
AND JULIA CHILD,
WHO LIT THE LAMP
AND SHOWED US
THE WAY

COOKING SCHOOLS

GREAT AMERICAN COOKING SCHOOLS

American Food & California Wine
Bountiful Bread: Basics to Brioches
Christmas Feasts from History
Romantic & Classic Cakes
Cooking of the South
Dim Sum & Chinese One-Dish Meals
Fine Fresh Food—Fast
Fresh Garden Vegetables
Ice Cream & Ices
Omelettes & Soufflés
Pasta! Cooking It, Loving It
Quiche & Pâté
Soups & Salads
Successful Parties: Simple & Elegant

ICE CREAM & ICES

NANCY ARUM

ILLUSTRATED BY ISADORE SELTZER

IRENA CHALMERS COOKBOOKS, INC. • **NEW YORK**

IRENA CHALMERS COOKBOOKS, INC.

PUBLISHER
Irena Chalmers

Sales and Marketing Director
Diane J. Kidd

Managing Editor
Jean Atcheson

Series Design
Helene Berinsky

Cover Design
Milton Glaser
Karen Skelton, *Associate Designer*

Cover Photography
Matthew Klein

Editor for this book
Margery Stein

Typesetting
J&J Graphics, Greensboro, NC

Printing
Lucas Litho, Inc., Baltimore

Editorial Offices
23 East 92nd Street
New York, NY 10028
(212) 289-3105

Sales Offices
P.O. Box 322
Brown Summit, NC 27214
(919) 656-3115

ISBN # 0-941034-07-0
Printed and published in the United States of America
by Irena Chalmers Cookbooks, Inc.

LIBRARY OF CONGRESS
CATALOG CARD NO.: 81-68842
    Arum, Nancy
        Ice cream and ices.

    Greensboro, N.C.: Chalmers, Irena Cookbooks, Inc.
84 p.
8108   810722

Contents

Acknowledgments

How many times have you heard people recall the days when ice cream cones cost a nickel? One's ice cream memories and experiences do often date back to childhood. It is not surprising, therefore, that I first give thanks to my parents and brothers for allowing my ice cream passion to surface.

Many a drive in Nellie Bell, our '53 Chrysler, included my pleas from the back seat to stop for ice cream. And sometimes, to my amazement, the car actually stopped—and out I ran. I still run for a good scoop!

Special thanks to Richard Burns, a New York-based chef who always made room for me and my ice cream machine wherever he worked through the years.

While some lent kitchens, others dished out encouragement. To Stewart Kampel, Rozanne Gold, Wendy Kyman and Susan Hardcastle, *merci*!

I am especially grateful to Libby Rosenthal, who helped gather some of the ridiculous and sublime data for this book.

Introduction

ICE CREAM. The mere words make my mouth water. And it's been that way for as long as I can remember. When I was exactly five years old, Congress passed a bill declaring my birthday Ice Cream Day—how appropriate!

The passion didn't subside with age. When I was in between owning and operating restaurants—one of which was a 1901 ice cream parlor complete with marble counter, brass foot rail, and beveled mirrors as a backdrop—I attended what I refer to as Ice Cream College. Actually, it was a two-week short course offered by Penn State University's College of Agriculture.

As I was preparing to leave, friends speculated that I would finally have my fill of ice cream. However, one week into the course, I found myself studying microbiology, which seemed unrelated to my fantasy of tasting the creamiest vanilla ice cream imaginable. And even though I didn't return with recipes for deep, dark, double chocolate ice cream, the diploma I received remains one of my proudest possessions.

My ice cream education was not wasted either. The following summer, two friends and I went into the ice cream business with our own manufactured ice cream, which we sold at street fairs from antique-looking ice cream carts. We called ourselves the Brooklyn Creamery. We're still friends—and we call one another when we've tasted or heard about a good scoop.

Perhaps the most enlightening part of my quest for the ultimate cold, sweetened, creamy taste that I so adore was realizing how easy it is to make my own ice cream. When I do make it myself, I experiment—add a dash more of rum, try a little less sugar—and still friends and family gobble up the results.

Often when I'm invited to somebody's house for a meal, I volunteer to make dessert, if they'll supply the ice. I carry my portable ice cream machine and create whatever appropriately goes with the meal or a seasonal specialty, like cranberry ice cream for Thanksgiving. People love it and really are amazed to be eating homemade ice cream, yet they've just witnessed how easy it is to prepare.

I've written numerous articles for newspapers and magazines describing the ease with which one can make ice cream with or without a machine. Finally, when the New School for Social Research in New York City developed a culinary arts department, I was invited to teach a course called, simply, Ice Cream, where I could praise the ease and virtue of homemade ices and ice cream.

And now I can continue to tell you about the advantages of making your own frozen desserts. Besides having total control over what goes into your ice cream—meaning nothing artificial—you can also begin to explore the countless combinations of flavors, textures, colors and fantasies.

The most wonderful thing about writing a book on ice cream is that every moment you're not at the typewriter—or in my case, testing recipes—can be called "research." So before I settled down to actually write this text, I took myself on a five-week trek to Europe.

It was a delicious trip. Though prune ice cream probably wouldn't make the top ten favorites in New York ice cream parlors, when the prunes are soaked in Armagnac, a subtle French brandy, and blended into a rich French vanilla ice cream, well . . . *C'est magnifique!*

In Italy I tried, with some trepidation, two new flavors—corn and rice. Again, I was surprised. Such "strange" ingredients tasted divine in frozen form.

Mainly I learned that one should try new combinations, experiment and, with an open mind and mouth, taste the results. And so, from the best of my taste memory, I hope to impart some of the wonderful and intriguing ices and ice creams I've known.

History

There was a time when you couldn't just go out to the corner store for ice cream, and history proves that I'm not the only person to take my frozen ambrosias seriously.

When the Roman Emperor Nero wanted a cool dessert, he ordered a general to deploy a team of runners to fetch snow from the Alps. The snow took a month to arrive back in Rome, where it was then flavored with fruit juices, honey and nuts. If too much of the snow had melted on its hot journey back to the emperor, the general in charge would have been killed—that's taking your sweet ices pretty seriously!

In the 13th century, Marco Polo expressed his devotion for frozen treats. Among the goodies he brought back from China were the formula for gunpowder, rare gems and recipes for a type of ice milk. In exotic Eastern lands, Polo reported, frozen delicacies were consumed as digestives following a meal of meat.

Soon, European armies were experimenting with gunpowder and Italian chefs were creating frozen feasts. The chefs developed a variety of dishes made with water, milk and cream. Some called the new product "cream ice" or "butter ice." Others, perhaps more romantically inclined, described it as "the flower of milk."

When 14-year-old Catherine de Medici moved from Florence to Paris to marry King Henry II, she brought a staff of chefs, and they brought their recipes for *gelati*—Italian for ice cream.

Throughout Europe, frozen desserts became the dishes of kings. Henry III of France, Catherine's son, ate ices every day. Louis XIV served "delicious sweetmeats" shaped like eggs that were "cold and compact as marble." King Charles I of England was so enraptured by a frozen cream ice—thought to be similar to

modern ice cream—that he declared the recipe a "royal secret" and paid his chef a yearly stipend to keep quiet.

Fortunately for posterity, Charles I was beheaded in 1649, and the word on ice cream was out. One story has it that a drooling group of English aristocrats purchased the secret from the late king's chef.

In the late 1600s, commoners finally had a chance to taste the royal treat. In 1670 a Sicilian named Coltelli introduced ice cream at his café, Le Procope, on Rue de l'Ancienne-Comédie in Paris, and patrons have been loving it ever since. Le Procope is reputed to be the oldest café in the world.

Swank ice cream parlors sprang up around Europe in the early 1800s, and another Italian named Tortoni became proprietor of yet another landmark Parisian café that served a rum ice cream mixed with almonds bearing the owner's name—Tortoni remains a popular dessert treat today. Perhaps this was also the start of the undying search for countless combinations of fruits, nuts and flavors.

Meanwhile, ice cream was taking off in what was to be its most fertile breeding ground: America.

In the United States, ice cream had already achieved unheralded status with a long list of fans. George Washington purchased a "cream machine for making ice," and spent $200 on ice cream one summer. Dolley Madison is known to this day for having served ice cream at White House state dinners. Thomas Jefferson gave his guests a dish he had tasted in France called *omelette surprise*—which we know as Baked Alaska.

But not everyone can dine at the White House, and in the early 1800s ice cream was still considered an exotic treat—hard to procure as well as to prepare.

During the summer months, ice was impossible to maintain. And the ice cream manufacturing method, which involved shaking a covered metal can of ice cream mixture in a bucket of salt and ice, was cumbersome, to say the least.

No wonder, then, that when Philip Lenzi's New York shop began to sell ice cream in 1774, customers had to put in advance requests. By 1777, Lenzi's store became even more exceptional by announcing that it now produced ice cream "almost every day."

In 1846 a woman named Nancy Johnson made life easier for the Philip Lenzis of the world by inventing a crude but easy-to-use hand-cranked ice cream maker. Although the Johnson invention certainly had a profound effect on posterity, she never patented the device—leaving others to become rich and famous.

One of those men who made money was Jacob Fussell, a milk dealer. With a very large supply

of cream, Fussell began the first U.S. ice cream factory in Baltimore in 1851. By 1864, he had plants in Washington, Boston and New York. Fussell's method still involved hand-cranking—which partly explains the astronomically high price of $1.25 per quart.

Other manufacturers soon entered the market, and by the late 1800s, America was addicted. "We dare not trust our wit for making our house pleasant to our friend," wrote Ralph Waldo Emerson, "so we buy ice cream."

As the industry boomed, hand cranks gave way to electric power and batch freezers to continuous freezing processes. One of Iowa's first ice cream moguls, F.D. Hutchinson, marveled when for one Fourth of July his workers labored to produce 300 gallons of ice cream. Today, some ice cream manufacturers churn out that volume in a matter of minutes.

By the 20th century, mere ice cream alone had become passé. But American ingenuity went to work and produced new, exciting variations—ice cream cones and ice cream sodas. And when moral guardians in Illinois decided that sodas were too sinfully good to serve on the Sabbath, soda jerks had to devise something without carbonation to serve their after-church customers. The solution? The so-called "Sunday soda"—thick syrup served over the ice cream. Its name was later changed to "Sundae" so as not to use the name of the Sabbath in vain.

The ice cream craze accelerated at the onset of Prohibition. With their old intoxicants banned, the people found a sweeter drug. As consumption skyrocketed, Christian Nelson of Iowa unveiled the Eskimo Pie in 1921, and the Burt family of Ohio patented the name Good Humor in 1923 for ice cream on a stick. And during these same Roaring Twenties we went full circle when an American named Paul J. Crawley began selling ice cream and Eskimo Pies at his store in

Shanghai—a far cry from the ice milk that Marco Polo had tasted in China 700 years before.

During World War II even government had to acknowledge ice cream's importance. In 1945, the Navy built a floating ice cream parlor to visit homesick soldiers. Ice cream, remarked Secretary of the Navy James Forrestal, was "more effective than beer in boosting morale."

For a number of years after the war, it seemed that ice cream was becoming a manufacturer's rather than a consumer's product. Factory size increased, synthetic flavorings multiplied and quality declined. A powerful ice cream lobby in Washington prevented consumers from finding out what their frozen fruit parfait ice cream actually contained. Jam makers had to list their ingredients, mayonnaise makers had to spell out their jar contents, and the same went for cereal suppliers. But ice cream manufacturers got away scot-free.

But on July 1, 1979, consumers scored a coup. Ignoring the pained cries of the ice cream industry, Congress declared that as of this date, all ice cream containers had to be printed with an ingredients list. And just in case some ice cream titan had any bright ideas, the law stipulated that contents must be listed in order of decreasing quantity: a "frozen dessert" that contains 1 percent cream cannot put "cream" at the top of its list. The bare facts must be plainly visible.

Happily, an increasing number of ice cream producers need not be ashamed of listing the contents of their product. According to *Ice Cream Field*, a trade publication, the quality ice cream market is booming, and fine frozen non-ice cream products—sherbets, sorbets and ices—are entering a renaissance. More important, the many ice cream fans who have recently discovered the delights of making their own frozen pleasures will never have to worry about reading ice cream cartons again.

In a sense, history repeats itself. Almost 2,000 years after the death of Nero, the world is once again enjoying ice flavored with just plain fresh fruit. And more than a century after Nancy Johnson's wonderful discovery, Americans are once again consuming ice cream made of cream, sugar, pure vanilla . . . and nothing more.

Ingredients

In an ideal world, where cost is not a consideration and ice cream is consumed soon after it is made, cream, sugar, natural flavorings and possibly egg yolks would be the primary ingredients in ice cream.

Today, however, the gallon of ice cream you pick up at the supermarket may contain any of an estimated 1,200 ingredients. If you are unlucky, or undiscriminating, you may pick up a carton of "ice cream" that contains no ice cream at all.

What are these 1,200 ingredients? Traditional ingredients aside, the list includes emulsifiers, artificial flavorings, stabilizers, artificial colorings and dairy by-products. Names like sodium alginate, polyoxyethylene sorbitan ester, and pyrophosphate may be unfamiliar to you, but if you've consumed a lot of commercial ice cream, chances are you've sampled them all.

Here now is a survey of ice cream components:

Cream.   Cream is used in the production of fine ice cream as a source of butterfat. But butterfat can be obtained from a variety of milk products. Heavy cream contains between 30 and 36 percent butterfat—though if you live on or near a farm, you can sometimes obtain cream whose butterfat content is as high as 45 percent; light cream contains between 18 and 20 percent; half-and-half between 10 and 12 percent, while the minimum fat content for milk in most parts of the country is 3 percent.

In the trade, the proud title of "Ice Cream" may only legally be bestowed upon products with a sufficient butterfat content. According to federal regulations, vanilla ice cream must contain 10 percent butterfat, while chocolate need only have 8 percent. Commercial brands stray considerably from these standards. The ever-popular Howard Johnson's comes on strong in the vanilla field with a butterfat rating of 16 percent; Bassett's shows a high of 16.5 percent for its French vanilla. At the other end of the scale is

another traditional brand—Dolly Madison, which a 1981 *Consumer Reports* revealed had an embarrassingly substandard butterfat rating of 8.5 percent. Respectable commercial ice cream (vanilla) should fall in the region of 12 percent butterfat content.

Cream is high in cholesterol, high in calories and expensive—a truly sinful delight. So how can you have your ice cream and eat it too?

If you make frozen desserts at home, you can keep your cholesterol intake as well as your costs down. Sherbets, devoid of cream, use egg whites or gelatin to maintain their smoothness; and homemade sherbets are delectable. Or you may want to make ice milk with less than 10 percent butterfat. Even avid ice cream fans will be dazzled by the rich taste that can be produced by using plain milk in the preparation of frozen desserts.

Do calories make you miserable? Ice milk, with only two-thirds the calories of the average ice cream, may again be the answer. But before you switch, remember that different ice creams vary tremendously in calorie count, and some quality ice creams are relatively low in calories. While Häagen-Dazs vanilla, rated "good" by *Consumer Reports* in 1981, contains a whopping 267 calories per serving, Friendly's vanilla, rated "excellent," contains a mere 134 calories.

Sweeteners. Butterfat, however, is not everything. Ice cream must, of course, be sweet. And nothing has yet been discovered that can completely replace sugar (sucrose) as an ice cream sweetener: it still accounts for 50 percent of the sweetener in all commercial ice creams. And what about the other 50 percent that are *not* sugar? At least part of the sweetness comes from less expensive goodies like hydrolized starch, dextrose, corn syrup and corn syrup solids. Sugar impostors can readily be detected

when used in excess—a "syrupy flavored" ice cream results.

Flavorings. There was a time when it was safe to say that strawberry ice cream was made with fresh strawberries, chocolate ice cream with cocoa, and vanilla ice cream with vanilla beans. Then came the chemical and processing revolutions. Today, most fruit ice creams are made with canned fruits or, even worse, no fruits—just artificial fruit flavorings with artificial coloring added. Most chocolates are concocted with an artificial cocoa-chocolate-liqueur blend. But the flavor that was hit hardest by modernization was the world's favorite—vanilla. Methylvanillan, the principal flavoring agent in the expensive vanilla bean, was found to be easy to synthesize. So what if the synthetic flavoring agent didn't taste quite like vanilla—it was close, wasn't it? And profits, not flavor, are the true bottom line of the ice cream industry. So—goodbye, natural vanilla.

But don't be duped. There are naturally flavored ice creams still around, and federal law

FLAVORINGS

requires that any so-called ice cream must fall into one of the following categories.

Category I must be flavored with natural flavoring agents, thus allowing it to be labeled simply and purely as vanilla ice cream or strawberry ice cream. Category II must owe its flavor to the natural flavor substance, but it may include flavor intensifiers or modifiers. On the supermarket shelf, containers of this middle-grade ice cream read, "Vanilla Flavored Ice Cream." Look carefully, and you'll find the words "artificial flavor added" lurking somewhere on the package's front panel. Only those so-called ice creams with more than 50 percent artificial flavoring are relegated to Category III. When you see a carton touting "Artificially Flavored Vanilla Ice Cream," you know it belongs to this last category. Always be sure you read with your eyes first before your tongue's judgment leads you astray.

Stabilizers. Even the name sounds unappetizing. Nevertheless, stabilizers are a necessary part of mass-produced ice cream.

Nero's snow made it from the Alps to Rome without melting. But the stockboys at the local supermarket have less at stake than Nero's runners, and the ice cream you purchase is probably not treated with Roman-style care. Modern ice cream frequently thaws in transit and is refrozen on delivery. In the trade, this trauma is called "heat shock." Ice cream with stabilizers survives the shock quite nicely, but "all natural" ice creams tend to develop ice lumps.

Many "all natural" ice creams are simply not well suited to stand up to the inevitable traumas that can occur on a very "unnatural" 500-mile trip from one part of the country to another. But of course, if the ice cream's longest journey is from your ice cream maker to your freezer, then stabilizers are irrelevant.

Emulsifiers. Emulsifiers, too, are modern innovations designed to meet modern commercial demands. Emulsifiers stiffen ice cream. Emulsified ice cream can hold more air—allowing for greater over-run (see page 19)—and can be more easily shaped into many wondrous frozen novelties. The world would not have mass-produced frozen neapolitan bricks or sleek rocket-shaped popsicles without the help of emulsifiers.

Still, some federal officials are not convinced of the benefit derived from adding, say, a glycerine emulsifier to hot fudge sundaes. But only one state, Alabama, has prohibited the use of emulsifiers in ice cream altogether.

Dyes. Those little black flecks in Philadelphia-style vanilla ice cream are natural—they're simply bits of the vanilla bean. But that rich yellow color of, for example, Baskin Robbins' vanilla, is 100 percent artificial. The color, which is supposed to suggest that there are egg yolks in

the ice cream—there are not—is produced by a dye called Yellow Dye Number 5, and some people are quite sensitive to the additive.

So, if you must buy commercial ice cream, read the labels and keep on your toes. Even when you see those darling shoppes with a hand-lettered sign hanging over the front door saying H*O*M*E*M*A*D*E I*C*E* C*R*E*A*M*, and your mouth begins to water, most often these nice folks are buying containers of premade ice cream mix—containing cream, milk (or both), sweetener, flavorings and often stabilizers and emulsifiers. They call the final product "homemade" because somebody on the premises pours the mix into the freezing machine. If he's creative, he may add some fresh fruit or nuts—but the consumer has little idea of what else may be in this ice cream.

Now you know what *can* be in your ice cream . . . but what *should* be there? That's a different question. I'll never forget meeting the highly respected Parisian caterer, Christian Constant, who worked for Lenôtre, the high priest of pastries, for 15 years before opening his dazzling shop on Rue du Bac—where his pastries and chocolates all but sparkle in the windows.

"I make ice cream the way my grandmother did," Monsieur Constant told me: "Eggs, sugar, cream and natural flavors—the best that I can find—and *c'est tout* (that's it). No big secrets."

Theory & Equipment

The theory behind making frozen desserts—whether in the million-dollar factory or the standing-room-only kitchenette—is deliciously simple. The cook takes a sweetened liquid mixture and freezes it. Cream or milk-based mixtures make ice cream, and those devoid of dairy products make ices.

If, for example, you take a mixture of sugar, water and pureed fruit and put it into an ice cube tray to freeze, you get a block of frozen fruit juice—a grown-up version of those cubes of frozen Kool-Aid that were colored sugar and water placed in a freezer.

But frozen desserts, both the smooth and fluffier types, require special care in freezing. In fact, the whole idea in making most sherbets and ice creams is to prevent the formation of intrusive ice blocks.

How's that done? Easy. If a mixture is stirred while freezing and the ice masses are rudely disrupted, the only remaining ice will be in the form of tiny crystals. The more the agitation, the slower the freezing, and the tinier the ice crystals. In some ice creams, the crystals are so small that you cannot detect their presence—"a wonderfully smooth ice cream," one might say.

Stirring also serves to aerate the ice cream. The mixing process fills the sweetened cream with tiny air pockets; without them a block of ice cream would be as easy to scoop as a rock.

Homemade ice cream naturally expands by approximately 25 percent during agitated freezing because of the incorporation of air. This increase is called over-run. In commercial ice cream plants, over-run is between 50 and 100 percent, because manufacturers pump air into their product without increasing costs. All too often, the economizing shows in the end product. A quart of store-bought ice cream is frequently only half as heavy as a quart of your own brand and half as rich and half as good . . . so why not make your own!

If you are now conjuring up images of yourself stirring an icy mixture for hours as it freezes, relax. Water ices, made in the freezer compartment of your refrigerator, require stirring only once an hour a total of two or three times. And modern technology has intervened with labor-saving devices for making sherbet and ice cream desserts that once required hours of icy agitation.

There are a wide variety of freezing devices, ranging from the cheaper hand-cranked versions you now find at flea markets and garage sales to the fancy new electronic devices (people who have invested in the latter are to be found selling the hand-cranked models at those sales).

But whichever you invest in, the principle is always the same. At the heart of the freezer is a metal can into which the ice cream mixture, which I will sometimes refer to as the recipe, is placed. Metal is a good heat conductor and allows the heat produced in the stirring process to escape.

There are a few details worth mentioning before you begin your first batch.

1. Read the instructions accompanying your ice cream machine carefully. Some will require kosher or rock salt while others simply need table salt.

2. Always clean the ice cream machine before using—in case the last person to use it didn't dry the canister well and rust stains remain behind.

3. Whenever possible, chill all equipment: bowls, egg beaters, blender or food processor bowl.

4. If the machine requires the old method of alternating layers of salt and ice, have lots of ice cubes made ahead of time. Also keep a supply of sponges and paper towels, and be sure to wipe off all the salt from the top of the canister after the ice cream has frozen. There's nothing worse than sweet vanilla ice cream with clumps of salt within.

ICE CREAMS

Introduction to Ice Cream

By now, you realize that I take my ice cream pretty seriously—seriously enough to divide it into categories. For our purposes, I've eliminated all ice cream recipes that in earlier days called for flour, cornstarch, gelatin and the like. That basically leaves us with French ice cream and Philadelphia ice cream.

The French style uses egg yolks and often has a greater proportion of milk to cream in the recipe. The Philadelphia ice cream is made without egg yolks and contains more cream than milk.

I prefer the Philadelphia style ice cream, which tastes cooler on my tongue. Also, I don't like the eggy taste I can detect in a French vanilla ice cream—although when a French custard base is used in a chocolate or coffee ice cream, the eggy flavor slides right past my taste buds. But I'm in the minority here. Most people prefer a French ice cream's rich, smooth and creamy texture and therefore find its flavor preferable.

Both the French and the Philadelphia ice creams have cooked bases; because of the addition of egg yolks in the French ice cream, its base is referred to as a custard. But if you find it too hot to turn on the stove, or you're too tired to cook a custard, you can still create wonderful homemade ice creams by merely mixing together cream, sweetener and flavorings right in the canister of your ice cream machine and freezing the mixture. This is especially recommended for those who happen to have a Guernsey cow in their pasture.

I'm not a devout believer that ice cream recipes must be followed to a T; feel free to experiment and get turned on to the ease of making others scream about your frozen concoctions.

Variations on Vanilla

While writing this book, I found myself in a dilemma. Because of my own passion for vanilla ice cream and my feeling that a good vanilla is the basis for all other ice creams, I could not decide which recipe to use for the best basic vanilla recipe. Finally, I decided to inundate you with several vanilla recipes and let you be the judge.

I know that there are chocolate ice cream aficionados, butter pecan nuts and strawberry maniacs—but I do see the world through vanilla-flavored glasses. You can create many wonderful flavors starting with this simplest of all—merely add fresh raspberries, chunky peanut butter, raisins soaked in rum or your favorite candy bar chopped up into bite-sized pieces. The possibilities depend only on your imagination and what tastes best to you.

Philadelphia Vanilla Ice Cream   *Makes 1½ quarts*

If you decide to use vanilla extract, buy only pure vanilla extract. The slightly cheaper synthetic vanilla flavoring, labeled imitation vanilla flavoring, should be banned—when frozen, it becomes obvious and obnoxious. Besides, why go to all the trouble of making your own ice cream and then impairing the final product with inferior ingredients?

1 quart half-and-half or light cream
1 cup sugar
½ vanilla bean, split lengthwise, or
   2 teaspoons pure vanilla extract

Heat the half-and-half with the sugar and vanilla bean in a heavy-bottomed saucepan, stirring frequently to dissolve the sugar. Do not boil. Remove the pan from the heat just before the mixture begins to boil, when tiny bubbles begin to form around the edge of the pan. Allow the mixture to cool to room temperature. With the sharp point of a paring knife, scrape the tiny seeds from the vanilla bean into the mixture. If using pure vanilla extract, add it to *cooled* mixture. Cover and refrigerate for at least 1 hour or preferably overnight.

Pour the cold mixture into the chilled canister of your ice cream machine and freeze according to the manufacturer's directions.

French Vanilla Ice Cream

Makes 1 quart

Vanilla beans are expensive, but they are so fragrant and easy to use that I hope you'll at least buy one and experiment with it. One vanilla bean can be reused several times—in between use, just wrap the split bean in saran or foil wrap.

Many people have fond memories of those little black specks—the seeds scraped from inside the bean—being an integral part of the vanilla ice cream experience.

2 cups milk
¾ cup sugar
Pinch of salt
½ vanilla bean, split lengthwise, or
    2 teaspoons pure vanilla extract
4 egg yolks
1 cup heavy cream, chilled

Heat the milk, ½ cup of sugar, salt and vanilla bean in a heavy-bottomed saucepan or the top of a double boiler, stirring frequently to dissolve the sugar. Do not boil.

Whisk the egg yolks with the remaining sugar in a mixing bowl. Still whisking, slowly pour in about a half cup of the hot liquid. When the mixture is smooth, slowly pour the egg mixture into the hot milk and continue whisking. Cook until just below boiling, when tiny bubbles form around the edge of the saucepan or when the mixture thickens slightly and coats the back of a spoon. Strain the custard into a metal or glass bowl and cool. With the sharp point of a paring knife, scrape the tiny seeds from the vanilla bean. If using vanilla extract, add it to the *cooled* custard. Cover mixture and refrigerate for at least 1 hour, or preferably overnight.

Stir heavy cream into the custard, pour contents into the chilled canister of the ice cream machine, and freeze according to manufacturer's directions.

The Easiest Vanilla Ice Cream

Makes 1½ quarts

Vanilla accounts for over one-third of all ice cream sales. Chocolate ranks second with 12 percent. Moving down the popularity list, we find neapolitan, chocolate chip, strawberry, vanilla fudge, butter pecan, cherry and butter almond.

Here's the easiest way to be in the majority.

**1 quart half-and-half, light or
 heavy cream
1 cup superfine sugar
2 teaspoons pure vanilla extract**

Combine the half-and-half, sugar and vanilla extract. Stir and pour contents into the chilled canister of your ice cream machine and freeze according to manufacturer's directions.

VARIATIONS

To make vanilla fudge, blueberry twirl, or butterscotch ribbon ice cream, simply prepare any of the vanilla ice cream recipes, freeze and place in a loaf pan in the freezer compartment of your refrigerator.

Make the sauce of your choice and when warm, not hot, pour a straight line of the sauce over the top of the hardened ice cream and gently cut the sauce into the ice cream with any household knife. Work quickly, otherwise it will be hard to distinguish the sauce from the ice cream and suddenly you will have chocolate instead of vanilla fudge.

Ultra-Rich Vanilla Ice Cream

If your cholesterol count can handle this one, you are in good health. This is the richest ice cream I've ever tasted and while I wouldn't make a daily habit of making this recipe, every now and again it's nice to know it's part of my repertoire. I save this for special occasions.

2 cups half-and-half
12 egg yolks
1 cup sugar
2 cups heavy whipping cream
1 whole vanilla bean, split lengthwise
½ cup butter (1 stick)
1 teaspoon vanilla extract (pure)

Heat half-and-half in a heavy-bottomed saucepan or the top of a double boiler to just under a boil, when small bubbles begin to appear along the edge of the pan. Cool, cover and refrigerate for at least 1 hour.

Cream egg yolks and ½ cup of the sugar, and set aside.

Heat heavy whipping cream, remaining sugar and vanilla bean in a heavy-bottomed saucepan, stirring frequently to dissolve the sugar. Do not allow to boil. When mixture begins to produce tiny bubbles around the edge of the pan, remove from heat and cool. Remove vanilla bean and with the sharp point of a paring knife, scrape the grains from the bean and mix into cream.

Pour about 1 cup of the sweetened cream mixture into the egg yolks, whisking constantly. Continue whisking and pour egg and cream mixture into a heavy-bottomed saucepan or double boiler. Heat to just under a boil, when tiny bubbles begin to appear at the edge of the pan.

Remove from heat and whisk in small pieces of butter until completely incorporated. Immediately place pan over ice to stop cooking, stirring frequently until cool. Strain through a fine sieve or strainer, add vanilla extract and beat in chilled half-and-half. Pour contents into the chilled canister of your ice cream machine and freeze according to manufacturer's directions.

Bittersweet Chocolate Ice Cream

Makes 1½ quarts

I once woke up and realized I knew the answer to running the finest restaurant in the world. Since I've owned two restaurants, have worked in many others and teach a course called "Demystifying the Ultimate Food Fantasy: Insights into Opening and Operating Your Own Small Restaurant," such a dream was not surprising.

The realization was merely to serve the best food possible by obtaining the finest raw ingredients and a superb chef to prepare and cook the food. Chocolate ice cream should operate on the same principle—find the best chocolate before proceeding with the following recipe, twice removed from Tom Kron, a chocolatier, whose chocolate I use in making this recipe.

1½ cups light cream or half-and-half
6 ounces bitter baking chocolate
1 can sweetened condensed milk
8 ounces semisweet chocolate
2 eggs
3 ounces rum (optional)
1½ cups heavy cream

Heat the light cream over a low flame in a heavy-bottomed saucepan or the top of a double boiler. Add the baking chocolate, stirring frequently until the chocolate dissolves completely. Gradually whisk in the condensed milk. Do not allow to boil.

In the top of a double boiler, melt the semisweet chocolate and add the warm cream mixture, stirring until thoroughly mixed. Cool to room temperature.

Whisk the egg and rum together with the heavy cream in a small mixing bowl. Slowly pour these ingredients into the cooled chocolate mixture and chill for at least 1 hour in the refrigerator. Mix and strain the chilled chocolate mixture into the chilled canister of your ice cream machine and freeze according to manufacturer's directions.

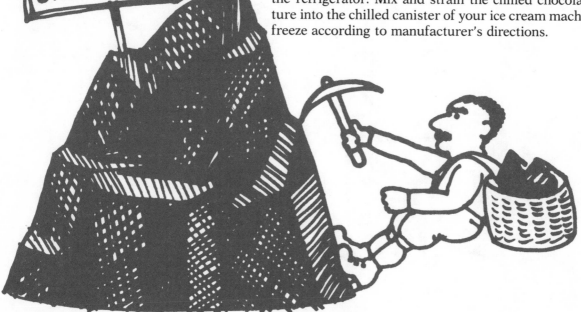

Swiss Chocolate Ice Cream

I like to use Lindt chocolate for this; when melted down, Lindt Excellence makes a delicious, smooth chocolate ice cream.

2 cups milk
6 ounces semisweet Swiss chocolate
1 ounce unsweetened chocolate
½ cup sugar
¼ cup water
Pinch of salt
3 egg yolks
1 teaspoon pure vanilla extract
1 cup heavy cream

Heat the milk with both chocolates in a heavy-bottomed saucepan or the top of a double boiler, stirring frequently until the chocolate is melted.

Heat the sugar and water in a small heavy-bottomed saucepan until it comes to a boil, about 3 or 4 minutes.

Whisk egg yolks and salt in a mixing bowl and slowly whisk in the sugar syrup. Continue whisking and gradually pour in warm chocolate milk. Add vanilla and heavy cream and refrigerate entire mixture for at least 1 hour.

Strain entire contents into the chilled canister of your ice cream machine and freeze according to manufacturer's directions.

Everyday Chocolate Ice Cream

Makes 1½ quarts

If you're making chocolate ice cream for 23 children, no one expects you to go out and buy expensive chocolate. For those occasions, here's a recipe using ingredients that can easily be obtained at the local supermarket. And to make the mundane truly memorable, Jeffrey Weisman, whom I met at New York City Community College's Hotel and Restaurant School, suggests pitting cherries and adding them.

2 ounces (2 squares) unsweetened chocolate
1 cup sugar
Pinch of salt
2 cups milk, heated
2 teaspoons pure vanilla extract
2 cups heavy cream

Heat the chocolate in the top of a double boiler, stirring frequently until it has melted. Add the sugar and salt and continue stirring. Whisk in the warm milk until the mixture is completely blended. Remove from heat, cool and add vanilla extract; refrigerate for 1 hour or longer.

Combine chocolate mixture and heavy cream and pour contents into the chilled canister of an ice cream machine. Freeze according to manufacturer's directions.

Coffee Ice Cream for Michele

Makes 1 quart

Michele Urvater, cookbook author and cooking school teacher extraordinaire, adores coffee ice cream, which makes sense since she spent her childhood in Belgium—good coffee is serious business there. According to Michele, nothing beats coffee ice cream—unless you pour a little bittersweet chocolate sauce over it. This recipe is a special thanks to Michele for her helpfulness.

½ cup coffee beans
2 cups milk
1 cup sugar
4 egg yolks
1 teaspoon pure vanilla extract
1 cup heavy cream, chilled

Preheat your oven to 350 degrees.

Roast the coffee beans for 5 minutes on a baking sheet or any large pan. When cool, grind the beans coarsely.

Heat the milk, ground coffee and ½ cup of sugar in a heavy-bottomed saucepan or the top of a double boiler, stirring until the sugar is dissolved. Strain the mixture to remove large coffee grains, but return the coffee mixture to the original saucepan and keep it warm over a low to medium heat.

Whisk together egg yolks and the remaining ½ cup of sugar in a mixing bowl. Still whisking, slowly pour in about ½ cup of the warm coffee mixture. When the mixture is smooth, slowly pour the egg mixture into the warm coffee mixture and continue whisking. Cook until just below boiling, when tiny bubbles form around the edge of the saucepan or when the mixture thickens slightly and coats the back of a spoon. Cool to room temperature, stir in vanilla and heavy cream and refrigerate for at least 1 hour.

Pour contents into chilled canister of ice cream machine and freeze according to manufacturer's directions.

Coffee Ice Cream

Rozanne Gold, once the chef for New York City's Mayor Koch, can certainly cook—but she can also make quite a strong cup of coffee.

Like most of us, Rozanne always has an extra cup of coffee hanging around her kitchen. Here's a recipe utilizing that leftover cup of coffee; just make sure it's a good strong brew.

1 cup coffee
3 cups half-and-half
1 cup sugar
Pinch of salt
1 teaspoon pure vanilla extract

Heat the coffee, half-and-half, sugar and salt in a heavy-bottomed saucepan or the top of a double boiler, stirring frequently to dissolve the sugar. Do not boil. Remove the pan from the heat just before the mixture begins to boil, when tiny bubbles start to form around the edge of the pan. Allow the mixture to cool to room temperature. Stir in the vanilla extract, cover and refrigerate for at least 1 hour.

Pour the cold mixture into the chilled canister of your ice cream machine and freeze according to manufacturer's directions.

Cappuccino Ice Cream

Makes 5 cups

My niece, Rebecca, once raved about a cappuccino ice cream featured as the flavor of the month in a Milwaukee dip shop she frequented. I guess it never made the best-hit list, as it was gone by the time I visited there. But no loss—I developed a cappuccino ice cream that Rebecca swears by.

1½ cups espresso
1 cup sugar
3 tablespoons freeze-dried coffee
1 cinnamon stick or 1 teaspoon
   ground cinnamon
2 tablespoons dark rum
2 cups heavy cream, chilled

Heat the espresso and sugar in a heavy-bottomed saucepan or the top of a double boiler, stirring frequently until the sugar is totally dissolved. Remove from heat and stir in freeze-dried coffee and cinnamon. Stir to dissolve the coffee and then allow coffee mixture to cool to room temperature. Add rum and refrigerate for at least 1 hour.

Remove cinnamon stick and add the heavy cream. Mix thoroughly and pour the contents into the chilled canister of your ice cream machine. Freeze according to manufacturer's directions.

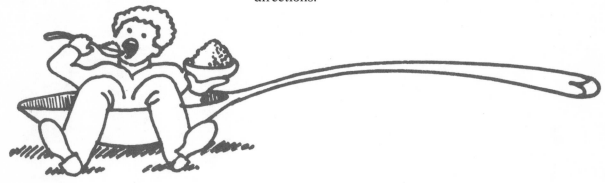

Fresh Raspberry Ice Cream

Makes 5 cups

In recent years, throughout the country, the pattern of ice cream consumption has changed drastically. Ice cream used to be America's favorite dessert; now it's our favorite snack. In 1967, 64 percent of ice cream families consumed it at dinner and 37 percent ate it at lunch. Today, the figures are 57 percent and 30 percent, respectively. The new ice cream prime time is late at night, when the midnight munchies strike.

One ice cream consumption statistic has remained stable throughout the other turbulent changes. In 1967 as in 1977, 1 percent of American ice cream households claimed to eat ice cream at breakfast—a habit, I suppose, not easily acquired or broken unless you try fresh raspberries and cream.

1 cup fresh raspberries
¾-1 cup sugar, depending on
   sweetness of raspberries
3 cups half-and-half
1 teaspoon lemon juice

Wash the raspberries and gently pat them dry with a paper towel. Place the berries in a bowl, mash and sprinkle with sugar. Let them sit for an hour at room temperature, tossing occasionally to make sure they are coated with sugar.

Mix the half-and-half, lemon juice and raspberries together and pour contents into the chilled canister of the ice cream machine. Freeze according to manufacturer's directions.

Frozen Blueberry Ice Cream

Makes 1 quart

When fresh berries are at the height of their season, they are ideal for adding to any of the basic vanilla ice cream recipes. When winter doldrums set in, a package of frozen strawberries, blueberries or raspberries becomes a wonderful reminder of warmer days ahead.

2 cups half-and-half
10-ounce package frozen
   blueberries, packed in syrup
Pinch of salt
1 teaspoon pure vanilla extract

Place all ingredients except the vanilla extract in the blender or food processor and blend until smooth. Heat the mixture over a low flame and simmer for 5 minutes, stirring frequently. Cool to room temperature, add vanilla, cover and refrigerate for at least 1 hour.

Pour contents into the chilled canister of your ice cream machine and freeze according to manufacturer's directions.

Cranberry Ice Cream

Makes 1½ quarts

Thanksgiving comes only once a year—which is unfortunate for me because it's the only time I can convince people that cranberry ice cream should be a permanent dessert item rather than a holiday oddity. I find the tartness of this all-American berry cuts the sweetness of the rich ice cream to near perfection.

2 cups cranberries
¾ cup water
1 cup sugar
3 tablespoons lemon juice
2 cups milk
1 cup heavy cream

Rinse cranberries, place them in a heavy-bottomed saucepan with the water, and heat over a low flame. Cook until tender, when soft and ready to pop. Press the berries through a sieve or puree them in an electric blender or food processor. Return the berries to the saucepan with the sugar and lemon juice, stirring until the sugar is dissolved. Remove from the heat and cool. Stir in milk and refrigerate for an hour.

Whisk heavy cream in a metal bowl until stiff, and gently but thoroughly fold into cranberry milk mixture. Pour contents into the chilled canister of the ice cream machine and freeze according to manufacturer's directions.

Rum Raisin Ice Cream

Makes 1 quart

While prune ice cream has not hit American shores (see next page), rum raisin has become a favorite on the East Coast and the West. Some commercial rum raisin ice creams are made with artificial rum flavoring that can too easily be detected. Made with a mere hint of rum hiding inside each plump raisin —that's a better way to concoct this somewhat subtle ice cream.

1 cup dark seedless raisins
¼ cup dark Jamaican rum
3 cups half-and-half or light cream
¾ cup sugar
1 teaspoon pure vanilla extract

Plump the raisins in the rum, preferably overnight.

Heat the half-and-half with the sugar in a heavy-bottomed saucepan, stirring frequently to dissolve the sugar. Do not boil. Remove the pan from the heat just before the mixture begins to boil, when tiny bubbles begin to form around the edge of the pan. Cool. Add vanilla extract, cover and refrigerate for at least 1 hour or preferably overnight.

Combine rum-soaked raisins and sweetened cream mixture, pour into the chilled canister of your ice cream machine, and freeze according to manufacturer's directions.

Peach Ice Cream

Makes 1 quart

Edna Lewis, an authority on Southern cooking, knows how to please people's palates. On a miserable, rainy night in March, the dessert Edna served was peaches. But not just any peaches. Edna had brought truly tree-ripened peaches from Virginia and soaked them in brandy and brown sugar for a while. You could eat these peaches plain, but now that I know Edna's sinfully delicious secret, I split the peaches in half and serve a large scoop of peach ice cream in between.

1½ pounds ripe peaches
2 tablespoons lemon juice
2 cups half-and-half
¾ cup sugar

Peel and pit the peaches, saving both the skin and pits. Coarsely puree the peaches with the lemon juice in a blender or food processor. Refrigerate the puree.

Heat the half-and-half with the skin and pits in a heavy-bottomed saucepan or the top of a double boiler over a low heat for 15 minutes. Do not boil. Add sugar, stirring frequently to dissolve the sugar completely. Strain the mixture into a glass or metal bowl. Cool to room temperature before refrigerating for at least 1 hour.

Combine sweetened half-and-half with peach puree and mix thoroughly. Pour contents into the chilled canister of the ice cream machine and freeze according to manufacturer's directions.

Prune-Armagnac Ice Cream

On a recent ice cream research trip to Europe I met Cynthia Frost, the first American and first woman to work in Lenôtre's kitchens at his school-factory in the Parisian suburb of Plaisir.

After a memorable meal minus dessert, Cynthia and I headed to the famed ice cream shop on the Ile St. Louis, where Monsieur Berthillon sells the frozen creations that are made next door. We tasted a good eight flavors, trying not to look at one another. Perhaps Cynthia thought I'd be influenced by her judgment—but the real reason I didn't look at her was that I didn't want her to see my disappointment. The vanilla was so-so, the chocolate not as densely rich as some I've had, and I've made better banana ice cream. But when the pruneaux glacés *arrived, and the prunes were soaked in Armagnac, a French brandy, I looked at Cynthia and the twinkle in her eyes confirmed my instinctive feeling that I had just tasted one of the best ice creams in my life. Try to forget every image you have about prunes and proceed with the following recipe.*

⅓ cup **Armagnac**
1½ **cups pitted prunes**
⅓ **cup water**
1 **cup sugar**
2 **cups milk**
4 **egg yolks**
Pinch of salt
1 **cup heavy cream**

Combine Armagnac, ⅓ cup of sugar and water in a heavy-bottomed saucepan and bring to a slow boil. Add the prunes and bring back to boil. Remove from heat, cover and allow prunes to steep in liquid for 1 hour, until cool. Pour mixture into a blender or food processor and puree until smooth. Reserve.

Heat the milk and ⅓ cup sugar in the top of a double boiler or a heavy-bottomed saucepan, stirring until sugar dissolves.

Whisk the egg yolks, salt and remaining ⅓ cup of sugar together in a mixing bowl, and slowly pour in about 1 cup of the hot sweetened milk, whisking constantly until smooth.

Return the yolk-milk mixture to the pan of sweetened milk and stir constantly until the mixture thickens slightly and coats the back of a spoon. Remove from the heat, strain into a glass or metal bowl and cool.

Combine custard and prune mixture and mix thoroughly. Add the heavy cream, pour the entire contents into the chilled canister of an ice cream machine, and freeze according to manufacturer's directions.

Avocado Ice Cream

Makes 1½ quarts

I often ask new restaurateurs what they did in their previous lifetimes. In America, one is usually not born into this business as is frequently the case in Europe.

Karen Hubert, owner-chef of Hubert's Restaurant in New York, was a poetess before taking her station behind the range. She applies much the same care in writing poems as in making frozen desserts.

Among the combinations she most enjoyed making were a blackberry-cassis sorbet served with a pear sherbet, coffee ice cream with chocolate chips, and ginger ice cream made with crystallized ginger.

One of Karen's particular favorites, however, was this sensationally rich avocado ice cream—for the adventurous!

3 cups heavy cream
¾ cup sugar
Pinch of salt
3 egg yolks
2-3 avocados
¼ cup Galliano

Heat the cream, sugar and salt in the top of a double boiler, stirring until dissolved.

Whisk the egg yolks in a mixing bowl, pour in a little of the hot cream and stir well. Gradually pour the egg mixture into the remaining hot cream and cook the custard, stirring constantly until slightly thick. Remove from heat and cool.

Peel and remove pits from avocados and puree in a blender or food processor. Measure 1 cup of pureed avocado. Mix avocado puree, Galliano and cooled custard together. Chill and pour into chilled canister of ice cream machine and freeze according to manufacturer's directions.

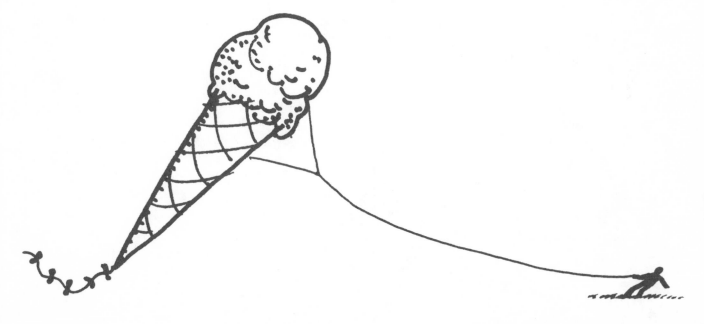

White Pistachio Ice Cream

Makes 1½ quarts

Once when I was writing an article on different people's favorite ice creams, Arthur Schwartz, editor of the "Good Living" section of the New York Daily News, *recalled a white pistachio ice cream manufactured by Louis Sherry Ice Cream Co., Inc.*

Since I had never tasted, seen nor heard of it, I decided to create a recipe; and of all the nutty ice creams—meaning, of course, ice creams containing nuts— this one is not only a refreshing treat but also a pleasant surprise, since it is devoid of food coloring and therefore white, not dyed green.

1 cup unsalted pistachio nuts
3 cups half-and-half
¾ cup sugar
4 egg yolks
Pinch of salt
1 teaspoon pure almond extract
1 cup heavy cream

Place a cookie sheet spread with shelled pistachio nuts in a 400-degree oven. Remove, cool and slip off skins.

Heat the half-and-half, ½ cup of sugar and the nuts in a heavy-bottomed saucepan or the top of a double boiler, stirring frequently until the sugar dissolves.

Whisk the egg yolks with the salt and remaining sugar in a mixing bowl.

Very slowly pour a thin stream of a cup of the hot liquid into the yolk mixture, whisking constantly until smooth. Pour the yolk mixture into the hot liquid, stirring frequently until it thickens slightly and coats the back of a spoon. Remove from heat and cool. Add almond extract and refrigerate for at least an hour.

Mix the heavy cream into the chilled custard, pour contents into the chilled canister of the ice cream machine, and freeze according to manufacturer's directions.

Real Maple Walnut Ice Cream

Makes 1½ quarts

Though pure 100 percent maple syrup commands a high price these days—even on the back roads where farms sell their very own syrup—the taste of maple walnut ice cream made with the real thing cannot be compared to the commercial varieties that use artificial flavoring.

1 cup pure maple syrup
2 eggs, slightly beaten
Pinch of salt
1 cup milk
2 cups heavy cream, lightly whipped
1 cup walnuts, chopped

Heat the maple syrup in the top of a double boiler but do not bring to a boil. Slowly add the slightly beaten eggs and stir rapidly until thoroughly blended. Remove from the heat and mix in salt and milk. Blend well. Cool. Add lightly whipped cream to the mixture, fold in walnuts, pour the contents into the chilled canister of the ice cream machine and freeze according to manufacturer's directions.

Peanut Butter Ice Cream

Makes 1½ quarts

Several years ago when I was visiting Laurie and Buck Johnson, my homesteader friends in upstate New York, their six-year-old daughter, Sarah, came dashing over to me with spoon in hand as soon as I walked into their cabin. We all had a good laugh when we realized that Sarah had gone to the cupboard and scooped out a spoonful of my favorite home-ground peanut butter—the coarse type with the peanuts that get caught in your teeth. So Sarah, my sweet, with you in mind, I combined my two favorite foods and came up with peanut butter ice cream—since bagel ice cream didn't have much taste.

1 quart half-and-half, light or
  heavy cream
1 cup chunky style peanut butter
1 cup sugar
1½ teaspoons pure vanilla extract

Combine the cream and peanut butter in a heavy-bottomed saucepan or the top of a double boiler, stirring constantly. Heat to just under a boil, until tiny bubbles form on the side of the pan. Add the sugar and continue stirring until dissolved. Remove from the heat, cool, add vanilla extract and chill in the refrigerator before placing contents in the chilled canister of an ice cream machine. Freeze according to manufacturer's directions.

Praline Ice Cream

You don't need me to teach you how to add M&M's or chopped-up Heath bars or any other candy to ice cream. I like to wait until the mix is almost frozen, then open the canister, remove the dasher and with a spatula blend in the candy. Replace the dasher and the top of the canister, and finish freezing.

But some candies, like sinfully sweet praline, are worth making yourself, especially if you want to tuck it into vanilla ice cream. Here's how.

1 cup sugar
⅓ cup brown sugar
⅔ cup water
1 cup pecans, toasted and chopped
4 cups half-and-half
Pinch of salt
1 teaspoon pure almond extract

Lightly butter or oil a cookie sheet and set aside.

Combine ½ cup sugar, ⅓ cup brown sugar and water in a heavy-bottomed saucepan over low heat until just below boiling, stirring constantly. The sugar will caramelize and become a light to medium brown color. Remove the pan from the heat and stir in the nuts. Return it to the heat and continue stirring until the syrup becomes a little darker. Be careful not to burn the mixture or it will be bitter.

Pour mixture onto prepared pan to cool. When cooled and hardened, crush by covering pan with wax paper and hammering it into pieces.

Heat the half-and-half in a heavy-bottomed saucepan to just below boiling, when tiny bubbles begin to form around the edge of the pan. Add remaining sugar and salt, stirring until sugar dissolves. Remove from heat, cool, add almond extract and refrigerate for at least 1 hour.

Pour contents into the chilled canister of the ice cream machine and freeze according to manufacturer's instructions. When the ice cream is partially frozen, open canister and fold pieces of praline into the ice cream, using a spatula. Cover canister and finish freezing ice cream.

Sherbets

Subtle—that's the word I associate with sherbets. Their colors often remind me of the tonal quality achieved by Impressionist painters: soft pinks, pale greens, delicate yellows and muted purplish-blues.

As a child, when faced with a long list of flavors at an ice cream shop, I would never listen to my cajoling brothers, who tried desperately to get me to order anything other than my favorite vanilla—except on a beastly hot day when we were off on a fishing trip and I knew I had another four hours in the back seat without air conditioning. During such dire circumstances I'd choose a cool, refreshing sherbet.

Sherbets fall under the large category of ices. Sherbets contain no cream. They are usually fruit flavored and made with either egg whites, milk or gelatin. If made with milk—I subcategorize these simply as ice milk—they use proportionately less milk, but often more sugar, than ice cream. I prefer to make sherbets with egg whites, but instead of 2 egg whites, feel free to use 1½ teaspoons of granulated gelatin that has been soaked in cold water and dissolved over hot water.

Sherbets can be made without a machine, but then you must be near your freezer several times a day to whisk the sherbets into their fluffy shapes.

Finally, when should you serve them—as a first course, in between courses to cleanse your palate, or as a grand finale? It's really up to you. If you do have leftovers, these homemade sherbets can stay in a freezer and be re-whisked into shape for a time, but I wouldn't suggest holding them longer than a month. The flavors tend to lose their vitality.

Still-Freeze Method

The still-freeze method of making frozen desserts requires neither churning nor a special ice cream maker. Sorbets and sherbets can easily be made in the freezer compartment of your refrigerator.

After mixing the ingredients called for in a recipe, simply pour the liquid into a shallow pan. An ice tray that has its dividers removed works very well and holds two cups of liquid perfectly. Place the pans or trays in the freezer until a broad rim of ice forms around the edge. This may take from one to three hours, depending on the coldness of your freezer. Stir the mixture once or twice during freezing.

Transfer the almost solid ice to a large chilled bowl and, using a sturdy fork, break the ice into smaller pieces. Then use a rotary or electric beater to whip ice into a mushy state. Put the beaten ice back into the pans or trays, cover with foil and refreeze to hardness. Repeat the whipping process again when it is partially frozen. For optimum smoothness, repeat a third time. The semifrozen ice can also be beaten in the food processor, but do chill the bowl and blade beforehand.

Citus Sherbet

Makes 1 quart

Frozen desserts seem to be the queen of American foods: 76.4 percent of U.S. consumers drink colas, 40 percent eat candy bars, and a whopping 91.2 percent indulge in ice cream, ice milk or sherbet.

Orange, lime and lemon head the list of favorites for sherbets, so I developed a basic citrus sherbet that can be used interchangeably. When making any of these sherbets, do use freshly squeezed citrus juices. And for orange sherbet, use 1¾ cups of orange juice plus ¼ cup of lemon juice.

1 cup sugar
1 cup water
2 cups freshly squeezed citrus juice
3 tablespoons grated rind from citrus
2 egg whites

Combine sugar and water in a heavy-bottomed saucepan and boil for 5 minutes. Remove from heat and cool.

Mix together cooled sugar syrup, citrus juice and rind and pour the contents into the chilled canister of the ice cream machine. Freeze according to manufacturer's directions, or follow still-freeze method.

When the sherbet is firm but not solid, beat egg whites until stiff. Fold them carefully but thoroughly into the sherbet and continue the freezing process.

Pink Champagne Sherbet

Makes 1 quart

When it comes to frozen desserts, America is Number One. This country today produces 44.08 pints of ice cream and related products per capita. That's 1.2 billion gallons altogether, which costs, when totalled, $2.763 billion. That's a long way from yesterday's 4,000 gallons a year—the standard set by this country in 1859.

Pink Champagne Sherbet was probably unheard of in the 1800s, but today such a treat can be made with a New York State champagne—of no significant vintage—to create a very soft pink sherbet. If you want to darken it slightly, just add a few tablespoons from the juice of sieved raspberries.

1 cup sugar
1¼ cup water
2 cups pink champagne, chilled
Juice of 1 lemon
2 egg whites

Dissolve the sugar in the water in a heavy-bottomed saucepan. Bring to a boil and let boil for 5 minutes. Cool and add champagne and lemon juice.

Beat egg whites until stiff and carefully but thoroughly fold them into the sweetened champagne. Pour contents into the chilled canister of an ice cream machine and freeze according to manufacturer's directions, or follow still-freeze method.

A Berry-Honey Sherbet

Makes 1 quart

I love a good argument, but I also cherish long-lasting friendships. So when it comes to the great debate of whether honey is better than sugar, I keep my mouth firmly shut.

Wendy Kyman, a friend since the days of The Magic Shop, my first restaurant and one of Manhattan's first natural food restaurants, is currently getting her doctorate in health education. She is also trying to raise her son, Jesse, with a health consciousness. So the least I can do when they come to visit is make sherbet with honey.

1 orange, juice and rind reserved
1 lemon, juice and rind reserved
4 cups strawberries, blueberries or
**   other ripe berries**
1 cup honey
½ cup hot water
2 egg whites

Grate the rinds of the orange and lemon. Reserve.

Puree the strawberries with the juice from the orange and lemon in a blender or food processor. Place the honey and hot water in a bowl, stirring until the honey dissolves. Add pureed berries and reserved grated rinds and mix thoroughly. Cool the mixture.

Beat the egg whites and carefully but thoroughly fold them into the sweetened berry mixture. Slowly spoon the mixture into the chilled canister of the ice cream machine and freeze according to manufacturer's directions, or follow still-freeze method.

Brandied Cranberry Sherbet

Makes 1 quart

I once covered a contest cranberry tasting and this recipe is adapted from that contest. It didn't win first prize, but I think it's pretty special.

4 cups cranberries
1½ cups water
1½ cups sugar
1½ cups orange juice
2 tablespoons brandy
2 egg whites

Rinse cranberries and place them in a heavy-bottomed saucepan with the water; heat over a low flame. Cook until they are tender—soft and ready to pop. Press the berries through a food mill or sieve, or puree them in a blender or food processor. Return the puree to the saucepan with the sugar and orange juice and stir until the sugar dissolves. Remove from heat, cool, stir in brandy and refrigerate.

Beat egg whites until stiff and carefully but thoroughly fold them into the sweetened chilled cranberry mixture. Place the contents in the chilled canister of an ice cream machine and freeze according to manufacturer's directions, or follow still-freeze method.

Blueberry Orange Sherbet

Makes 1 quart

This tasty dessert can be made with frozen, unsweetened blueberries. If using fresh ones, go through the pint-size baskets and be a little discriminating, tossing out any molded or rotten blueberries.
    Serve the sherbet in the hollowed-out halves of the oranges after squeezing them for their juice.

⅔ cup sugar
1 cup water
3 cups blueberries
1 cup fresh orange juice
¼ cup fresh lemon juice
2 tablespoons Grand Marnier or other
  orange liqueur
2 egg whites

Heat the sugar and water together in a heavy-bottomed saucepan and bring to a boil. Boil for 5 minutes. Remove from heat and cool.

Wash and pat dry fresh blueberries and puree in a blender or food processor. You will probably have a little less than 2 cups of puree.

Combine blueberries with orange and lemon juice and liqueur. Add the sugar syrup and mix thoroughly. Beat egg whites until stiff and carefully but thoroughly fold into the blueberry-orange mixture. Slowly spoon contents into the chilled canister of an ice cream machine and freeze according to manufacturer's directions, or follow still-freeze method.

Pink Grapefruit Sherbet

Makes 1 quart

I like to serve grapefruit sherbet in between courses at a winter fete. It tends to be a little on the tart side. That may surprise some guests, but as a trou de milieu *or palate refresher—as the French refer to a spoonful of such cold cleansers—it's a delight. Try it before carving and consuming a roast or bird to remove the taste memory of previous dishes.*

1 pink grapefruit, unpeeled and cut
  into 1-inch pieces
2 cups water
1 cup superfine sugar
½ cup fresh grapefruit juice
2 tablespoons fresh lemon juice
2 egg whites

Wash the grapefruit skin well and cut it into 1-inch pieces. Heat the grapefruit in a cup of water in a heavy-bottomed saucepan until tender, about 10 to 15 minutes. Pour contents plus ½ cup of sugar into a blender or food processor with the metal blade and puree fruit. Return sweetened grapefruit puree to the saucepan and simmer slowly until thick, stirring frequently. Remove from heat, stir in grapefruit juice and allow the mixture to cool.

Combine the remaining cup of water with ½ cup sugar in a small saucepan and boil for 5 minutes. Remove from heat and cool.

Combine cooled sugar syrup and grapefruit puree with lemon juice.

Beat egg whites until stiff and carefully but thoroughly fold into grapefruit mixture. Slowly spoon contents into the chilled canister of an ice cream machine and follow manufacturer's directions, or follow still-freeze method.

Pineapple Sherbet
Makes 1 quart

Feeling lazy? Open a can of unsweetened pineapple and then see what else you have around. Flavor it with rum or kirsch or combine the pineapple with raspberry or apricot puree before freezing. If you're serving Chinese or Indian food, consider making the sherbet au naturel.

1 cup unsweetened pineapple juice
½ cup water
1 cup sugar
**2 cups unsweetened crushed canned
  pineapple**
3 tablespoons lemon juice
2 tablespoons rum or kirsch (optional)
2 egg whites

Heat the pineapple juice, water and sugar in a heavy-bottomed saucepan, stirring frequently until the sugar has dissolved. Boil for 5 minutes. Remove from heat and cool. Mix in pineapple, lemon juice and rum and refrigerate.

Whisk egg whites until stiff, and slowly but thoroughly fold them into the chilled pineapple mixture; carefully spoon contents into the chilled canister of an ice cream machine and freeze according to manufacturer's directions, or follow still-freeze method.

Rhubarb Sherbet

If you planted rhubarb in your garden, you may be out of ideas for what else to do with the huge quantities that always seem to arrive at once. Rhubarb jam, strawberry-rhubarb pies and stewed rhubarb have probably been on the menu more than once. When I had rhubarb sherbet in Paris, I couldn't wait to try it back home. It's a little tart, so I serve it between courses or with some sweet madeleine cookies.

**2 cups cooked rhubarb,
approximately 2 to 3 pounds**
1 cup sugar
1 cup water
1 tablespoon fresh lemon juice
¼ cup vodka
2 egg whites

Bring sugar and water to a slow boil in a heavy-bottomed saucepan. Boil for 5 minutes. Remove from heat and cool.

Remove the leaves and rough ends of the stem on the rhubarb, cut stalks into small, 2-inch pieces and place in a heavy-bottomed saucepan with water to cover. Cook over a low to medium heat until tender. Drain and puree rhubarb in an electric blender or food processor and cool.

Add cooled rhubarb puree, lemon juice and vodka to the sugar syrup and mix thoroughly.

Whisk egg whites until stiff and gently but thoroughly fold them into the rhubarb mixture. Carefully spoon contents into the chilled canister of an ice cream machine and freeze according to manufacturer's directions, or follow still-freeze method.

Cantaloupe Sherbet

If my mother's kitchen had been a restaurant, it would have been called The Two—not Four— Seasons. Dinners would most often begin with half a grapefruit, except when melons were ripe. At those times a slice of cantaloupe was the order of the day.

Picking out a good melon is certainly part of the secret of making a good cantaloupe sherbet; my father, who did and still does enjoy shopping, taught me to examine the stem end of a melon to see if it is slightly sunken and rough and therefore ripened on the vine, not picked before its time. Also, he smells the melon for sweetness. Now I do the same, and you should too.

1 cup sugar
1 cup water
2 cups cantaloupe puree or other
   melon in season (approximately
   1 medium melon)
2 tablespoons rum (optional)
2 egg whites

Dissolve the sugar in the water in a heavy-bottomed saucepan. Bring to a boil and let boil for 5 minutes. Remove and cool.

Remove the rind and seeds from the melon and puree it in an electric blender or food processor. Chill. Combine melon puree and sugar syrup and mix well. Add rum.

Beat egg whites until stiff and carefully but thoroughly fold them into the sweetened melon mixture. Slowly spoon the mixture into the chilled canister of an ice cream machine and freeze according to manufacturer's directions, or follow still-freeze method.

Pear Sherbet

Makes 1 quart

In August 1977, Bennett D'Angelo set a world record for eating ice cream. He consumed three pounds six ounces in 90 seconds at Dean Dairy in Waltham, Massachusetts. Perhaps if his frozen dessert had been made with fresh Bartlett pears I could comprehend this feat. The texture from pureed Bartlett pears would make anybody swallow such nectar—maybe even in the quantities Mr. D'Angelo achieved.

2 pounds Bartlett pears
3 tablespoons fresh lemon juice
½ cup sugar
⅔ cup water
1 cinnamon stick or 2 teaspoons
   cinnamon
2 egg whites

Wash, peel, cut pears in half and remove seeds, cores and stems. Slice and sprinkle them with lemon juice and sugar. Let pears stand at room temperature for at least 30 minutes, tossing pears occasionally.

Heat the pears, water and cinnamon stick in a heavy-bottomed saucepan over low to medium heat for approximately 15 minutes, or until pears are tender.

Remove cinnamon stick and puree pears with water in blender or food processor. Cool and refrigerate.

Whisk egg whites until stiff and gradually but thoroughly fold into the chilled pear mixture. Slowly spoon contents into the chilled canister of an ice cream machine and freeze according to manufacturer's directions, or follow still-freeze method.

Peachy Tomato Sherbet

Makes 1 quart

How many times have you said or heard a mother say, "Don't turn up your nose until you've tried it," when trying to convince a child to taste something new. Well, even I'll admit some combinations are a little weird. But vine-ripened tomatoes usually appear on the farm stands about the same time as juicy peaches, so to me, the pairing of tomatoes and peaches seems quite logical. When I serve this sherbet to strangers, I usually make them guess the flavor.

1½ pounds ripe tomatoes
2 pounds ripe peaches
1 cup water
¾ cup sugar—can add more if
**   mixture is not sweet enough**
2 tablespoons gin
2 egg whites

Bring a large pot of water to a rolling boil and immerse the tomatoes and peaches in it for 1 or 2 minutes. Remove and immediately immerse them in cold water. Drain, skin and slice the peaches. Skin, core and slice the tomatoes. Combine tomatoes, peaches and the cup of water in a heavy-bottomed saucepan. Bring to a slow boil and cook for 15 minutes, until peaches are tender. Remove from heat and puree in blender or food processor. Stir sugar into puree until dissolved. Cool, add gin and refrigerate.

Whisk egg whites until stiff and slowly but thoroughly fold into chilled peachy tomato mixture; carefully spoon contents into the chilled canister of an ice cream machine and freeze according to manufacturer's directions, or follow still-freeze method.

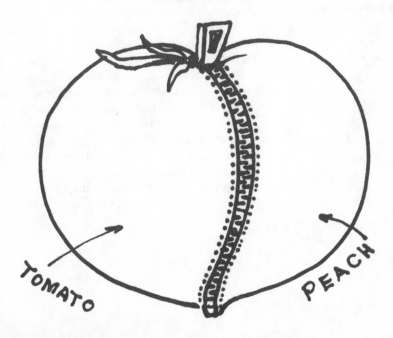

Mango Sherbet

Makes 1½ quarts

Tropical fruits were unknown to me until my brother married a woman from Bogotá, Colombia. If you've never tasted a mango, you're in for an ethereal experience. It is rich and sweet but never cloying. When made into a frozen dessert, the bright orange mangoes are magnificent. Use only ripe mangoes whose yellowish skin—often speckled with red or black—yields slightly to gentle pressure.

¾ cup sugar
¾ cup water
3 cups mango puree (5 or 6 medium mangoes)
3 tablespoons fresh lemon juice
2 egg whites

Dissolve sugar in water in a heavy-bottomed saucepan. Boil for 5 minutes. Remove and cool.

Hold the stem end of the mango in the palm of your hand and, with a sharp knife, cut through the skin from top to bottom in several places. Peel the skin down as you would with a banana. The mango seed is long and flat and the flesh clings to the seed, so it is best to slice flesh from seed lengthwise. Puree the mango through a food mill, blender or food processor. Combine mango puree, lemon juice and sugar syrup and mix well.

Whisk the egg whites and gently but thoroughly fold them into the sweetened mango mixture. Carefully spoon contents into the chilled canister of the ice cream machine and follow manufacturer's directions, or follow still-freeze method.

SORBETS
&
GRANITAS

Sorbets

The first piece of journalism I ever did was for the *New York Post*. It started out, "I love ice cream more than most people . . . . " I'd revise it now and say, I love ices, or more specifically sorbets, more than most people—but that's because most Americans don't know how good sorbets can be.

Sorbets are those ices made simply and purely with fruit puree or fruit juices plus a sugar and water syrup. They have achieved a new status in this country since the introduction of nouvelle cuisine—an uncomplicated method of preparing lighter foods that emphasizes the simple taste of the freshest ingredients. Many French restaurants present an assortment of sorbets in a rainbow of colors as a dessert. The variety is unending, and I hope, once again, you will experiment with your own combinations of fruit, liqueurs and even vegetables.

Because fruits can vary so much in sweetness, I suggest you taste the recipes; they should be slightly sweeter than you want because when they are frozen, the intensity of the flavor decreases.

Strawberry Sorbet
Makes 1 quart

This is the first sorbet I ever made, and it has remained a favorite. When strawberries are in season, it should be a favorite of yours too. Its color is quite eye-catching, its taste delectably refreshing. And when you see how easy it is to make, you won't want to make any other dessert—especially in the hot weather.

2 pints fresh strawberries
⅔ cup sugar
1 cup fresh orange juice
¼ cup fresh lemon juice
¼ cup Grand Marnier or other orange liqueur

Wash and hull strawberries. Gently blot them dry with a paper towel. Place berries in a bowl, mash and sprinkle with ⅓ cup sugar. Allow the berries to sit at room temperature for at least a half hour. Toss frequently.

Heat the remaining sugar with the orange and lemon juice in a heavy-bottomed saucepan, stirring until the sugar dissolves. Remove from the heat and cool.

Puree the berries in a blender or food processor. Be sure the sugar that sinks to the bottom is mixed into the pureed berries.

Combine berries with sweetened juices and stir in the liqueur. Follow the still-freeze method for this recipe.

Apple Sorbet

For the past few years New Yorkers have been blessed with the Green Markets. Every day except Monday from June through the fall, designated areas throughout the city become marketplaces where farmers come from upstate, Long Island and other nearby areas to sell their produce—all of which has been picked within 24 hours of market time. For many city dwellers, it's the next best thing to having one's own plot of land. In the fall, each market is perfumed with apples and fresh cider.

1½ cups apple cider
½ cup sugar
2 pounds apples, ripe and firm
¼ cup lemon juice, freshly squeezed
2 tablespoons applejack
Pinch of cinnamon

Heat the apple cider with the sugar in a heavy-bottomed saucepan, stirring until the sugar dissolves. Remove from heat and cool.

Wash, pare, core and slice apples and place in a heavy-bottomed saucepan with enough water to cover. Cook over low to medium heat for 10-15 minutes, until soft. Drain and discard water.

Puree apples in a food mill, blender or food processor. Strain through a fine-mesh sieve, discarding skins and fibers. Cool and combine with sweetened apple cider, lemon juice, applejack and cinnamon. Pour contents into the chilled canister of an ice cream machine and freeze according to manufacturer's directions, or follow still-freeze method.

Kiwi Sorbet

Within the United States, a healthy interstate ice cream rivalry exists. Californians will be pleased to note that their state leads the pack, producing 11 percent of the nation's supply. Pennsylvania, home of wonderful Bassett's, is next in line with 9 percent. But Philadelphians, who contend that quality is more important than quantity, are turning up their noses at the West Coast competition.

The first kiwi fruit I ever saw was in the Los Angeles Farmer's Market. After tasting one, I decided it would make a marvelous sorbet because of its gorgeous green color contrasting with its own tiny black seeds.

1 cup water
1 cup sugar
8 kiwi fruit
2 tablespoons fresh lemon juice

Heat sugar and water in a heavy-bottomed saucepan. Bring to a boil for 5 minutes, remove from heat and cool.

Peel the kiwis and puree them in a food mill, blender or food processor. Mix puree with the sugar syrup and lemon juice and place contents in the chilled canister of the ice cream machine; freeze according to manufacturer's directions, or follow still-freeze method.

Three-Citrus Sorbet

Lest the United States become lax in its devotion to ice cream, let it be known that several other countries have almost equally adoring fans. In Australia, 42.05 pints of frozen desserts are produced per person each year, and in New Zealand the figure is 37.3 pints. At the opposite end of the scale are countries like Egypt, Indonesia and the Ivory Coast. Your average Indonesian may only have .03 pints of ice cream a year—how he must suffer!

½ cup sugar
½ cup water
1 cup fresh grapefruit juice
1½ cups fresh orange juice
½ cup fresh lemon juice
Grated rind from 2 lemons
Grated rind from ½ grapefruit

Heat the sugar and water in a heavy-bottomed saucepan. Simmer for 5 minutes, remove from heat and cool.

Combine the fruit juices, grated rinds and cooled sugar syrup and pour contents into the chilled canister of the ice cream machine; freeze according to manufacturer's directions, or follow still-freeze method.

Carrot-Dill Sorbet

Makes 1 quart

Before I had tasted one, the idea of a vegetable sorbet seemed ridiculous. It wasn't, as I realized immediately when I tried one, and now I enjoy thinking up new vegetable combinations to make into sorbets. When Richard Burns was the chef at Vanessa's restaurant in Greenwich Village, he tasted my carrot-dill sorbet and immediately put it on the menu to be served with a bowl of cold gazpacho. Besides being a taste treat, the color combinations delight the eye.

1½ **cups fresh orange juice**
½ **cup sugar**
1 **pound carrots**
¼ **cup fresh lemon juice**
1 **tablespoon vodka (optional)**
2 **tablespoons fresh dill**

Heat orange juice with sugar in a heavy-bottomed saucepan, stirring until sugar dissolves. Allow to boil 5 minutes. Remove from heat and cool.

Wash and scrape carrots and remove bitter ends. Cut into 2-inch pieces, place in a saucepan with water to cover and cook 15 minutes, or until tender. Drain and puree carrots in a food mill, blender or food processor. Cool.

Combine sweetened orange juice, pureed carrots, lemon juice and vodka and spoon contents into the chilled canister of an ice cream machine; freeze according to manufacturer's directions, or follow still-freeze method. When the mixture is almost frozen, stir in the fresh dill and continue freezing. Cut the dill in small pieces with scissors for best results.

Gazpacho Sorbet

Noted food consultant Barbara Kafka opened some pretty special doors for me when I made the switch from restaurateuring to writing. I've kept in touch with Barbara, and there's always something special cooking in her kitchen.

Recently, Barbara and her staff worked on the recipe book for Simac's Il Gelataio, The Ice Cream Man. Here's one of Barbara's favorite recipes for a summertime treat when the garden is overflowing with large ripe tomatoes.

2½ cups chilled gazpacho (recipe
    follows)
2 tablespoons fresh lemon juice
2 teaspoons kosher salt
1 cup water
1 cup tomato juice
¼ teaspoon Tabasco sauce
4 grindings of fresh black pepper

Mix all the ingredients together, adjusting the seasonings to taste. Strain the mixture and reserve the vegetable chunks. Pour the liquid into the chilled container of the ice cream machine and freeze according to manufacturer's directions, or follow still-freeze method. After 10 minutes of freezing, stir in the reserved vegetables and freeze until firm.

GAZPACHO

½ medium-size Bermuda or other
  sweet white onion, peeled
  and quartered
1½ firm, medium-size cucumbers,
  peeled and cut into chunks
2 small green peppers, seeded and
  cut into eighths
6 medium-size to large ripe
  tomatoes, peeled and cut into
  eighths
5 large garlic cloves
1 cup tomato juice, approximately
½ cup light olive oil
¾ teaspoon chili powder or 1 small
  piece fresh chili pepper
1 tablespoon kosher salt

Add the onion to the work bowl of a food processor fitted with the metal blade. Process, turning on and off rapidly until finely chopped, about 4 or 5 seconds. Transfer the onion to a large bowl.

Repeat with the cucumbers, then with the green peppers, adding each to the onions in the bowl. Process 5 of the tomatoes until evenly chopped into small pieces. Transfer to the bowl with the other chopped ingredients.

Process the remaining tomato with the garlic, tomato juice, olive oil and chili powder until a smooth liquid is formed. Combine with the chopped vegetables and salt and chill in a covered container.

Honeydew Melon Sorbet

Restaurants have taken advantage of sorbets' spectacular colors and often present three egg-shaped balls on a large white dinner plate surrounded by thin slices of fresh fruit, sprigs of mint or whole fresh berries. Since it's true that we eat with our eyes first, why not present several sorbets at your home as well.

If you make the following honeydew melon sorbet, there will be several slices of honeydew left after pureeing the fruit. Save them for presenting with a strawberry or orange sorbet, as their light green color contrasts well with other fruits.

1 large honeydew melon
3 tablespoons fresh lime juice
1 cup sugar
1 cup water
¼ cup dry sherry

Peel and seed the honeydew melon. Cut the melon into slices and then into 1-inch cubes and puree in a blender or food processor until you have 3 cups of puree. Place the puree in a bowl and add the lime juice.

Meanwhile, heat the sugar and water in a heavy-bottomed saucepan and let boil for 5 minutes. Remove from heat and cool.

Combine cooled sugar syrup, melon puree and sherry and pour contents into the chilled canister of the ice cream machine; freeze according to manufacturer's directions, or follow still-freeze method.

Apricot Sorbet

Makes 1 quart

Are you familiar with those dried apricots sold in health food stores—the ones without the sulphur, that look shriveled up and inedible? They're an unappetizing brown color. Well, they taste much better than they look, and when fresh apricots aren't at the nearest fruit stand or budding on your backyard tree, this dried variety will suffice—rather nicely, too.

1 cup sugar
1 cup water
2 cups dried apricots
1½ cups fresh orange juice
1 cup apricot nectar
2 tablespoons fresh lemon juice
¼ teaspoon grated lemon rind
¼ teaspoon grated orange rind

Heat sugar and water in a heavy-bottomed saucepan. Simmer for 5 minutes. Remove from heat and cool.

Combine dried apricots with orange juice over low heat in a heavy-bottomed saucepan, stirring occasionally to insure that apricots do not stick to the bottom of the pan. Simmer approximately 20 minutes, or until apricots are soft. Puree apricots in a food mill, blender or food processor. Cool.

Combine cooled apricot puree with sugar syrup, apricot nectar, lemon juice and grated rinds from the lemon and orange.

Pour contents into the chilled canister of the ice cream machine and freeze according to manufacturer's directions, or follow still-freeze method.

Easy Orange Sorbet

Makes 1 quart

Even in major ice cream eating countries, ice cream production is in a bit of a slump. Production in New Zealand actually dropped 9 percent in 1979. In America, the percentage change hasn't been that great, but production in 1980 was down 50 million gallons from its high in 1975. And with increased mechanization, fewer people and a smaller number of factories are involved in making the product commercially.

In 1947, 29,300 people worked in the industry. Though production has doubled today, only 11,300 are so employed. In 1963, 2,493 plants made ice cream. By 1979 the number had dwindled to 990.

Though some commercial titans moan at the shrinkage of the industry, we do-it-yourself ice cream optimists have something to celebrate. The decreasing number of factories suggests that a growing number of small restaurants and individuals are saying "Down with mass production" and are making their own ice cream.

When making a frozen dessert is as easy as opening a carton of orange juice, how can you not make your own?

1 quart orange juice

You can simply pour the contents of a carton of orange juice into the chilled canister of the ice cream machine and

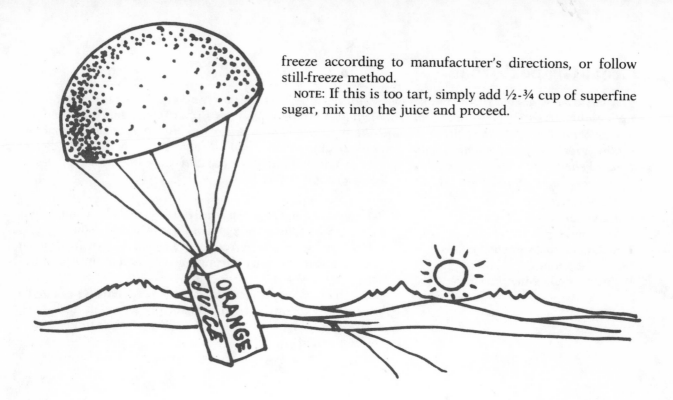

freeze according to manufacturer's directions, or follow still-freeze method.

NOTE: If this is too tart, simply add ½-¾ cup of superfine sugar, mix into the juice and proceed.

Beet Sorbet

Makes 1 quart

I have an undying passion for beets. Their regal color excites me and their sweetness has always surprised me. When served with borscht, a beet soup that has sour cream mixed in, the deep magenta of the beet sorbet in the almost-shocking-pink cold soup will win over the most complacent dinner guest.

1 pound beets
3 cups water
2 tablespoons fresh lemon juice
¼ cup brown sugar
¼ cup sugar
Pinch of salt

Cut the leaves and stems off the beets, wash, slice and peel beets and place them in a saucepan with the water, lemon juice, sugars and salt. Place over a low to medium heat and cook for 30 minutes or until beets are tender. Reserve liquid.

Puree the beets through a food mill, blender or food processor. Cool and refrigerate along with the reserved liquid.

Place the beets and liquid in the chilled canister of an ice cream machine and freeze according to manufacturer's directions, or follow still-freeze method.

Great Grape Sorbet

You might be surprised to learn that some countries in Europe that are well known for ice cream are not among the major producers. France and Italy, with their delicious frozen treats, only produce 9.2 and 11.02 pints per person, respectively. And although England produces 7.85 pints of ice cream per person per year, 6.45 of those pints are non-dairy ice cream. Where does non-dairy ice cream get its fat content? Well, Wall's, one of England's major ice cream producers, actually manufactures two products—ice cream and sausages. The rest I leave to your imagination.

1 cup water
¾ cup sugar
2 pounds seedless purple grapes
Juice of 2 lemons
¼ cup Marsala wine

Heat water and sugar in a heavy-bottomed saucepan. Simmer for 5 minutes. Remove from the heat and cool.

Mash the grapes or puree them in a blender or food processor. Strain the juice through a fine sieve, removing the skins.

Combine grape juice, cooled sugar syrup, lemon juice and wine and pour into chilled canister of ice cream machine; freeze according to manufacturer's directions or follow still-freeze method.

Papaya Sorbet

In 1969 Bruno Belilty, a pharmacist in the fashionable 16th arrondissement in Paris, had many well-heeled female customers who were constantly concerned and complaining about their weight. Yet at lunch time, when the pharmacist went to the nearby and well-known Brasserie Stella, he noticed many of these same women finishing their light lunches with ice cream sundaes topped with whipped cream, nuts and cherries.

After Belilty had mentioned this curiosity to his friend Jacques Guipon, then the director of the brasserie, the two men decided to make a cool, sweet, all-natural dessert that would have fewer calories. They experimented with sorbets using exotic fruits—mangoes, guavas, kiwi and passion fruit. Now they produce 1,000 liters per day under their label La Sorbetière.

1 cup water
¾ cup sugar
6 ripe papayas
½ cup fresh lime juice

Combine water and sugar in a heavy-bottomed saucepan. Simmer for 5 minutes, remove from heat and cool.

Peel papayas and remove black seeds. Cut papaya into cubes and puree through a food mill, blender or food processor. Immediately add lime juice to papaya puree. Combine papaya-lime puree with cooled sugar syrup.

Pour contents into the chilled canister of the ice cream machine and freeze according to manufacturer's directions, or follow still-freeze method.

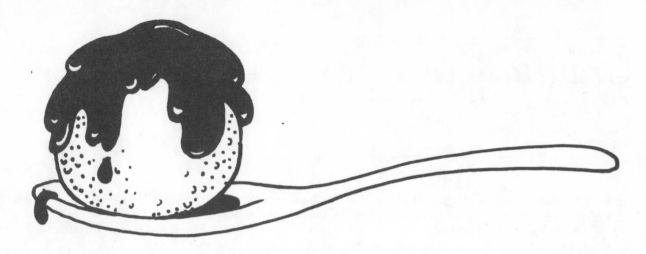

Chocolate Orange Sorbet

Makes 1 quart

It's a sobering reality to finally realize that you truly cannot please everyone. However, in the world of food, it seems silly not to try. The ultimate challenge for me is pleasing my nine-year-old twin nieces. They love to make me prepare two different breakfasts or different vegetables. But when I experimented and combined chocolate and oranges, I had no complaints from the younger generation.

3 ounces unsweetened chocolate
3 cups water
1 cup sugar
½ cup fresh orange juice
½ teaspoon grated orange rind
¼ teaspoon pure vanilla extract

Chop the chocolate into tiny pieces, using a sharp knife or a food processor.

Heat the water and sugar in a heavy-bottomed saucepan or the top of a double boiler. Add the chocolate and simmer for approximately 15 to 20 minutes, until the mixture is very smooth. Remove from heat and cool.

When cool, mix in orange juice, rind and vanilla extract. Pour contents into the chilled canister of the ice cream machine and freeze according to manufacturer's directions, or follow still-freeze method.

Granitas

In Italy, granitas are coarsely textured ices. No machine is required, since their rough texture is best achieved when made by the still-freeze method. Be careful not to beat the semifrozen ice often, as that breaks down the large ice crystals, which you want for a true granita. I simply stir the icy mixture with a sturdy fork two or three times during the freezing process.

While any of the granitas recipes can be made into a sorbet and vice versa, the recipes I've chosen tingle one's tongue in the loveliest manner because of their sharp texture. You'll never know what I'm talking about unless you try it.

Cranshaw Melon Granita
Makes 1 quart

While writing this book, I frequently had neighbors knocking on my door to ask how things were going. Sometimes, I suspected they were curious to see if I was busier at the typewriter or churning the ice cream machine. My next-door neighbor, Susie, not only listened to all my woes about my prose but also used her taste palate, as opposed to her painter's palette, to help judge the better recipes for this book. This one, with its soft orange color, was a favorite.

1 Cranshaw melon
⅔ cup superfine sugar
¼ cup framboise

Peel and remove the seeds from the melon. Slice, and cut into 1-inch cubes. Place cubed melon pieces in a blender or food processor; switch the machine on and off frequently but do not puree finely. In other words, it's okay if it's lumpy.

Mix lumpy melon puree with sugar and framboise. Pour contents into a shallow pan (or 2) and place in the freezer compartment. When icy, remove and with a sturdy fork sort of whip or beat the ice crystals to move them around. Replace in freezer and repeat the process after it freezes a little more.

Red Wine Granita

Makes 1 quart

There are many aficionados—or better yet, frozen dessert freaks—who love to talk about their sweet addictions. But whenever I meet people in the wine business, their jargon seems to involve a little more than just the percentage of butterfat. Anyway, I became friendly with the people who own Kenwood Winery in the Sonoma area of California after I wrote a story about art on wine labels. For Christmas one year, Marty Lee sent me a bottle of their red table wine, which I sampled. With half the bottle left, I made a red wine granita that can be made with a burgundy, beaujolais or whatever is left over from dinner the night before.

1 cup water
¾ cup sugar
¼ cup applejack
Pinch of salt
1 cinnamon stick
2 cups red wine
1 tablespoon fresh lemon juice
1 tablespoon grated lemon rind

Heat water, sugar, applejack, salt and cinnamon stick in a heavy-bottomed saucepan. Simmer for 5 minutes, remove from heat and cool.

Remove the cinnamon stick from the cooled sugar syrup and add wine, lemon juice and lemon rind. Chill in the refrigerator for at least 2 hours before pouring contents into shallow pans and placing in freezer. Follow still-freeze method but do not whip the ice crystals too smoothly. Granitas should have a coarse texture.

Coffee Granita

When a holiday occurs in Italy, all the shops shut their doors and have a day of rest ... that is, except for the ice cream purveyors. In Bologna one religious holiday, I wandered through the streets wondering if I'd find a restaurant open. Instead, on a small street I saw people flocking to a little shop where a woman was scooping up granitas in a fabulous array of colors. I opted for a coffee granita and I chose well, as it had a strong, sweet flavor. There, it is served with a dollop of freshly whipped cream. You may want to serve it similarly, at the end of a perfect meal.

1 cup water
1 cup sugar
1 cinnamon stick
2 tablespoons grated lemon rind
3 cups espresso coffee, chilled
1 tablespoon Kahlua liqueur, optional

Heat the water, sugar, cinnamon stick and lemon rind in a heavy-bottomed saucepan. Simmer for 5 minutes. Remove from heat and cool. Remove cinnamon stick.

Add chilled espresso to sugar syrup and refrigerate for at least 2 hours. Add coffee liqueur and pour the contents into shallow pans; follow still-freeze method for granitas.

Campari-Grapefruit Granita

Makes 1 quart

When I first began writing for the suburban sections of The New York Times, *I had to "audition" for the position. The editor sent me to review a restaurant on Long Island and instructed me to take three other people with me. Of course, I decided to take friends who had a good knowledge of food and also wouldn't mind my tasting their meal.*

So I called up Jerry Jacobson, who has traveled throughout Europe in search of a good meal and fine wine. His well-trained palate is enhanced by his knowledge of food. His extensive collection of cookbooks is not merely for show; Jerry reads them with a real passion.

Jerry introduced me to Campari, an aromatic liqueur made from quinine and other unknown ingredients. Italians drink it straight on the rocks and Americans doctor it with club soda. It is said to be good for what ails you—a good digestive. I love it mixed with grapefruit juice.

Small can frozen grapefruit juice
2 cups water
¼ cup Campari
Superfine sugar to taste, if you must

Dilute the can of frozen grapefruit juice with 2 cups of water and the Campari and pour into a chilled loaf pan or ice cube trays. Follow the still-freeze method for a coarsely textured end result.

If you or your guests find this granita too tart, superfine sugar will help.

Watermelon Granita

Patricia Soller, an executive chef for a private Wall Street dining room, has cooked for a living in restaurants, test kitchens and classrooms for a number of years. Quantities never seem to unnerve her. So if she's planning to feed four, it wouldn't faze her if 40 more came to the table. She's just calm about feeding people.

When dessert has to be served, Patricia likes to put out a tray of ripe cheeses and a bouquet of fresh fruits that may vary from the exotic to the mundane. Once there was half a watermelon left over from one of her sumptuous meals. I agreed to take it home and made what I call my all-American granita. Removing the seeds from the melon is the most time-consuming part of this recipe.

**Half a watermelon, approximately
   4 pounds**
1 cup water
½ - ¾ cup sugar
2 tablespoons fresh lemon juice

Remove the rind and seeds from the watermelon. Slice the melon into 1-inch cubes and mash it with a knife, or puree coarsely in a blender or food processor. Refrigerate.

Heat the water and sugar in a heavy-bottomed saucepan. Simmer for 5 minutes; remove from the heat and cool.

Combine the watermelon puree (you should have about 2½ cups), sugar syrup and lemon juice. Refrigerate for at least 1 hour. Pour into shallow pans, place in the freezer and follow still-freeze method for granitas.

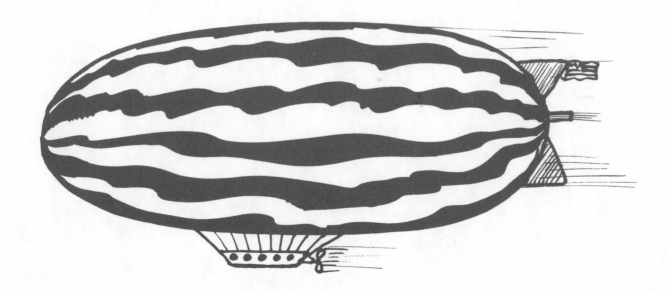

ICE MILKS & FROZEN YOGURT

Ice Milks

Ice milks are sometimes referred to as sherbets or milk sherbets. But if a frozen dessert is made with milk instead of cream, plus flavoring and sweetener, I call it an ice milk. The first spoonful of ice milk melting down your tongue may surprise you, as it tends to be very cold and to refresh the taste buds in a way unlike ice cream desserts, which are made with heavy cream and egg yolks.

Most soft-serve ice cream and "softies" sold from stands and vans are made from ice milk mixtures, which are less expensive because of the exclusion of cream.

Ice milk's biggest plus for calorie-conscious consumers of frozen delights is the fact that it is lower in calories and cholesterol. But whether you use 99 percent fat-free milk, skim milk, non-fat dry milk, or homogenized milk in your recipes, ice milk can be as exciting as your flavorful imagination allows.

Vanilla Ice Milk   *Each makes 1 quart*

Ice milks, in addition to being low in calories, are extremely easy to make. Those two pluses should be sufficient incentive for giving these frozen treats a fair chance.

Here are two basic recipes; you can add nuts or fruit purees to them, depending on your tastes.

**4 cups whole milk or 99 percent
   fat-free milk
1 cup superfine sugar
1½-2 teaspoons pure vanilla extract
Pinch of salt**

Pour ingredients directly into the chilled canister of your ice cream machine; freeze according to directions.

VANILLA II

**3 cups skim milk
½ cup sugar
6 tablespoons non-fat dry milk
2 teaspoons pure vanilla extract**

Heat the milk, sugar and non-fat dry milk in a heavy-bottomed saucepan, stirring until the sugar and dry milk are dissolved. Remove from heat and cool thoroughly. Stir in vanilla and pour the mixture into the chilled canister of your ice cream machine; freeze according to directions.

Chocolate Ice Milk

Makes 5 cups

If you are adding fruits or nuts to ice milk recipes, freeze the mixture for a while, stop the machine to fold in the extra goodies, and finish freezing. Peanuts, almonds and/or raisins give chocolate ice milk a whole other dimension—one well worth considering.

4 cups whole milk or 99 percent
  fat-free milk
½-¾ cup superfine sugar
½ cup chocolate syrup or
  6 tablespoons cocoa
1 teaspoon pure vanilla extract
½ teaspoon ground cinnamon
Pinch of salt

Pour ingredients into the chilled canister of the ice cream machine and mix well before freezing according to manufacturer's directions.

CHOCOLATE II

Makes 1 quart

1 quart milk
1½ cups sugar
4 ounces unsweetened chocolate

Heat the milk and sugar together in a heavy-bottomed saucepan, stirring until the sugar dissolves.

In the top of a double boiler, melt the chocolate over low heat, stirring until smooth. Continue stirring and slowly add the sweetened milk mixture to the chocolate. Cook until smooth. Cool thoroughly and refrigerate for at least 1 hour before pouring the mixture into the chilled canister of the ice cream machine and freezing according to manufacturer's directions.

Strawberry Ice Milk

Makes 1 quart

Here are several different ice milks. Choose any one of them using any variety or combinations of berries you happen to have.

2 cups strawberries
½ - ¾ cup sugar, depending on sweetness of berries
1½ cups milk
½ cup fresh orange juice
⅛ teaspoon cinnamon
1 tablespoon lemon juice

Wash and hull the strawberries. Gently dry them. Mash the berries and place them in a heavy-bottomed saucepan with the sugar and heat them over a low flame for approximately 10 minutes. Puree them in a blender or food processor, strain and cool.

Combine the cooled berry mixture with milk, orange juice, lemon juice and cinnamon and pour the contents into the chilled canister of the ice cream machine; freeze according to manufacturer's directions.

Blueberry Ice Milk

Makes 1 quart

2 cups skim milk
⅔ cup sugar
6 tablespoons non-fat dry milk
1 teaspoon pure vanilla extract
2 cups blueberries
1 tablespoon fresh lemon juice

Heat the milk, ⅓ cup of the sugar and non-fat milk in a heavy-bottomed saucepan, stirring constantly. Remove from the heat and cool.

Wash the berries and cook them with the remaining sugar in a heavy-bottomed saucepan over a low flame, for approximately 10 minutes. Puree the berries in a blender or food processor, strain and cool.

Combine the cooled milk with the blueberries, vanilla extract and lemon juice and pour the contents into the chilled canister of the ice cream machine; freeze according to manufacturer's directions.

NOTE: If you are using a 10-ounce package of frozen berries packed in syrup, simply thaw the berries, puree them in a blender, add 2 cups of milk and a teaspoon of lemon juice and pour the mixture into the chilled canister of the ice cream machine; freeze according to manufacturer's directions.

My Dreamsicle Creamsicle

Makes 1½ quarts

At least 9.5 percent of America's milk goes into making frozen desserts. While the frozen dessert category includes several products, ice cream alone accounts for 67 percent of frozen dessert production—still America's favorite. Ice milk makes up 25 percent of production, sherbet 3.7 percent, water ices 2.6 percent and imitation ice cream, called "mellorine," 1.3 percent of production.

When you open a carton of milk and mix it with orange juice, freeze it and create memories of Creamsicles on a stick, I'd think ice milk production would skyrocket.

3 cups whole milk
2 cups fresh or 100 percent pure
   orange juice
1-1½ cups superfine sugar
Pinch of salt

Mix ingredients together and pour into the chilled canister of the ice cream machine. Follow manufacturer's directions for freezing.

Minted-Lime Ice Milk

This is a favorite of mine because of its tingling tartness. To make it less tart, you can add two or more tablespoons of green crème de menthe.

**1 cup freshly squeezed lime juice
(about 8 limes)**
1 cup superfine sugar
Pinch of salt
2 cups milk
Grated rind of 2 limes
2 tablespoons green crème de menthe

Combine lime juice, sugar, salt, milk, grated lime rinds and crème de menthe. Pour into the chilled canister of the ice cream machine and freeze according to manufacturer's directions.

Frozen Yogurt

Few Americans had heard of frozen yogurt in 1976, but within two years it had cornered approximately 6 percent of the frozen dessert market—and 75 percent of all ice cream manufacturers were making it.

Danny frozen yogurt on a stick was introduced in supermarkets a decade ago, but it was not until the arrival of soft frozen yogurt that the concept caught on. Titans of the frozen dessert industry were elated: they had finally broken what industry insiders call "the snack barrier"—the reluctance that women between the ages of 18 and 35 have about consuming sweets.

Yet the fact is, frozen yogurt is no low-calorie wonder. Although the original Eastern European yogurt, with its sour lactic acid taste, is genuinely dietetic, the yogurt that we eat today is, to quote *Dairy Field Magazine*, "third generation." After the sweeteners and artificial fruit flavors are added, today's commercial frozen yogurt contains about the same number of calories as ice cream.

Many frozen yogurts are made artificially—leaving out the "live bacteria cultures" that are the very essence of true yogurt. These live bacteria are what make the yogurt so healthful; they also give it its characteristic sour taste, which manufacturers cover up with lots of sugar. Manufacturers also, for convenience, have eliminated live cultures by a process called "direct acidification." The acid gives their yogurt a sourish taste but has little nutritional value. Fortunately, many state legislatures have become wise to the direct acidification sham, and in many parts of the country direct acidification products cannot be called "yogurt." Since the average consumer is unable to check the labels on yogurt cartons whose liquid goes into the frozen yogurt machine, you're better off making your own.

Berry Frozen Yogurt

Makes 1 quart

Frozen yogurt can be made at home with chunks of fresh fruits and honey, keeping it the healthy treat it was first meant to be.

2 pints fresh strawberries
2 cups plain yogurt
⅓ cup honey or ¼ - ½ cup sugar

Wash, pat dry and hull the strawberries. Puree the berries in a blender or food processor and mix in the yogurt and sweetener. Mix thoroughly and pour contents into the chilled canister of the ice cream machine; freeze according to manufacturer's directions.

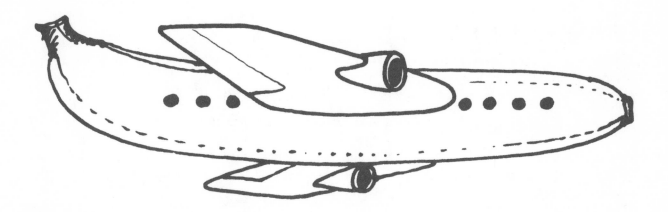

Banana Frozen Yogurt

Makes 1 quart

Strawberry is the favorite commercial frozen yogurt flavor, accounting for 39 percent of sales, and raspberry is a strong second at 34 percent—but at home my favorite flavor is banana.

2 bananas, very ripe
½ cup dark brown sugar
1 tablespoon fresh lemon juice
1 quart plain yogurt

Mash the very ripe bananas with a fork and sprinkle lemon juice and brown sugar on top. Let the mixture stand at room temperature for approximately 30 minutes, tossing it occasionally to make sure the sugar is mixed throughout the bananas.

Thoroughly mix in the plain yogurt and refrigerate for 1 hour. Pour contents into the chilled canister of the ice cream machine and freeze according to manufacturer's directions.

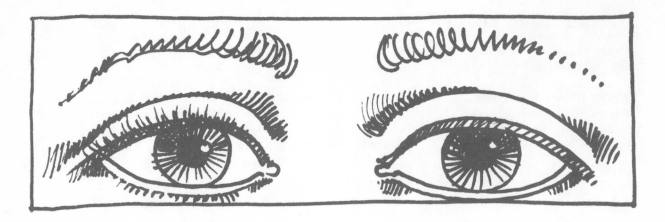

Irish Coffee Frozen Yogurt

Makes 1 quart

Anybody who owns a restaurant should have at least one Lea Nielsen. She was my right arm, my conscience, adviser—and a whole lot more—during my restaurateuring days. She had the patience of a saint when a customer couldn't decide among chocolate decadence, an ultra-rich, moist cake or a scoop of Irish coffee ice cream . . . her favorite, though she didn't indulge often enough. But that's past history, and now I have developed an Irish coffee dessert without all the butterfat . . . for everybody's indulgence.

3 cups plain yogurt
½ cup superfine sugar
¼ cup freeze-dried coffee
2 tablespoons Irish whisky

Combine all the ingredients together and mix well. Taste. If it's not sweet enough, add more sugar. Pour contents into the chilled canister of the ice cream machine and freeze according to manufacturer's directions.

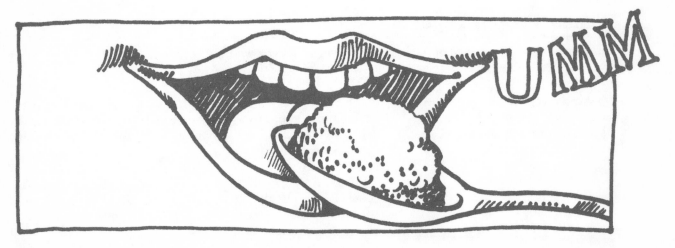

FROZEN
COCKTAILS

Frozen Piña Colada

My childhood friend Richard Brause grew up to be, among other things, a great frozen margarita-maker—not such a bad avocation on hot, humid days in New York City. I once attempted to freeze some margaritas in my ice cream machine. It worked fairly well—that is, if you like frozen margaritas. I discovered I don't, but I went on to freeze fruitier alcoholic drinks.

1 20-ounce can pineapple
1 cup coconut cream
1 teaspoon lemon juice
Dash salt
Dash bitters
1 cup water
1 cup rum

Drain the pineapple—which can be in slices, crushed or other form—and puree the fruit in a blender or food processor. Mix the pineapple with the remaining ingredients and pour into the chilled canister of the ice cream machine; freeze according to manufacturer's directions.

Frozen Banana Daiquiri

My father's a good cook. He used to make great potato pancakes for Sunday morning breakfasts. Every summer there'd be the usual family barbecue with overcooked hamburgers, rubbery hot dogs, and syrupy-sweet baked beans. Nobody ever seemed to care about the food, however, as long as my father was making his famous frozen daiquiris. I asked him more than once for the recipe, but I could never get a straight answer because he never made it the same way twice. I've since watched more closely; the fruits he uses vary—strawberries, bananas or a mixture of melons—or, as he says, "whatever I find at the market." Whichever fruit you choose, be sure it's ripe.

3 ripe bananas
½ cup fresh lemon juice
¼ cup brown sugar
1 cup rum
½ cup superfine sugar
¾ cup water

Peel and mash bananas with a fork or puree in a blender or food processor, with lemon juice and brown sugar. Let the mixture sit at room temperature for about 10 minutes.

Add rum, superfine sugar and water and puree well in the blender or food processor. Pour contents into ice cube trays or a loaf pan and place in the freezer. Follow the still-freeze method.

If you are using melon or berries, use 2½ cups of fruit puree, ½ to ¾ cup of superfine sugar, ½ cup fresh lemon juice and 1 cup of rum.

SAUCES
& SUCH

Chocolate Sauce

I have never figured out why people put cloyingly sweet syrups, gooey nuts, fluffed-up whipped cream and dyed cherries on top of something as delicious as a scoop of ice cream. But they do—and you might too—so I've included some homemade toppings for you to try.

If you put out dishes of freshly made vanilla ice cream with a selection of sauces, freshly whipped cream, a myriad nuts, crushed fruits, and other goodies like sprinkles and M&M candies, the end result is inevitably the same: the chocolate sauce—whether the hot fudge variety or the not-so-clingy type—always gets gobbled up first.

¼ cup butter
2 squares (2 ounces) unsweetened chocolate
1½ cups sugar
Pinch of salt
¾ cup heavy cream
½ teaspoon pure vanilla extract

Melt the butter and chocolate in the top of a double boiler or in a heavy-bottomed saucepan, over a very low heat. While stirring, add the sugar slowly. Continue stirring and add salt; slowly pour in the cream. Cook until the sugar dissolves, approximately 5 minutes. Remove from the heat, and add vanilla.

To turn this into a mocha sauce, simply add 2 tablespoons of freeze-dried coffee to the above recipe.

No-Fuss Chocolate Sauce

To the basic chocolate sauce you can add 2 tablespoons of grated orange rind and ¼ cup of orange juice for a chocolate-orange sauce.

To make an almond chocolate sauce, add 1 cup of toasted slivered almonds and ½ teaspoon pure almond extract.

Add mint extract with crushed peppermint candy, if that's a taste you enjoy.

Some people just like a simple, smooth chocolate sauce and don't want to fuss about it.

8 ounces of your favorite semisweet or milk chocolate
1 cup heavy whipping cream

Melt the chocolate in the top of a double boiler and stir. While stirring, slowly add the cream. When it reaches the consistency you desire, remove it from the heat and serve hot, or let it cool to room temperature.

Bittersweet Chocolate Sauce with Orange Peels

Makes 1½-2 cups

There's only one sauce that I ever thought was worth tasting with a good vanilla ice cream: a bittersweet chocolate sauce with orange peels floating in it. I've tried, to the best of my taste memory, to duplicate it for you.

2 squares (2 ounces) semisweet cooking chocolate
¾ cup water
1 tablespoon sugar
Pinch of salt
1 tablespoon butter
2 tablespoons orange rinds, thinly sliced

In the top of a double boiler, heat chocolate and water. While stirring, add sugar, salt and butter until creamy. Stir in rinds. Serve hot.

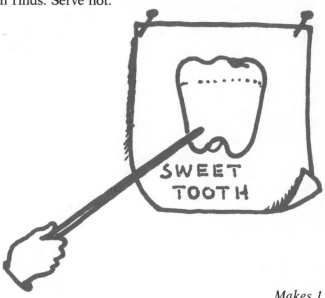

Butterscotch Sauce

Makes 1 cup

Here's another favorite for those with a sweet tooth.

½ cup light corn syrup
½ cup dark brown sugar
2 tablespoons butter
Pinch of salt
¼ teaspoon pure vanilla extract
¼ cup heavy cream

Heat the corn syrup, brown sugar, butter and salt in the top of a double boiler or in a heavy-bottomed saucepan, stirring constantly. When the mixture is just about to boil and has thickened, remove it from the heat and cool.

Stir in the vanilla and slowly mix in the cream. This sauce can be served hot or cold and reheats beautifully in a double boiler.

Caramel Sauce

Caramel sauce is nothing new. A cookbook I have that dates back to 1896 had a recipe for this sweet sauce, and it's basically the same one I've always used.

1 cup sugar
¾ cup hot water
½ teaspoon vanilla

Heat the sugar in a heavy pan over a low flame, stirring constantly. The sugar will turn brown (caramelize) in approximately 10 minutes. When it's light brown, begin to slowly add the water. Add vanilla and boil approximately 5 more minutes. Remove from the heat and cool.

You can substitute ¼ cup of black coffee for ¼ cup of the water for a slight variation.

Blueberry Sauce

When I made soups from scratch, as well as desserts and quiches, at my second restaurant, I remember customers raving about the iced tea I served. I felt like a mother whose child wouldn't eat after she had slaved behind a hot stove all day.

A similar experience occurred in an ice cream course I taught. There I was giving out ultra-rich recipes for the chocoholics and lovers of vanilla ice cream. One man came up to me after class to tell me that the easy blueberry sauce recipe alone was worth the price of the course!

3 cups fresh blueberries
½ cup sugar
1½ teaspoons cinnamon
½ teaspoon freshly grated nutmeg

Combine all ingredients in a heavy-bottomed saucepan. Cook for approximately 10 minutes over low heat, stirring frequently. Serve hot or cold.

No-Fuss Fruit Topping

To make a no-fuss fruit topping, take crushed fruits —peaches, strawberries, raspberries or blueberries—and mix them with sugar. Use 4 parts of fruit to 1 part sugar. Thus for 2 cups of fruit, mashed to an agreeable consistency, sprinkle ½ cup of sugar, tossing occasionally. Let the sweetened fruit marinate for a day in the refrigerator for best results—but it can be served immediately.

Apricot Sauce

1 cup dried apricots
1 cup orange juice
1 teaspoon grated orange rind
16-ounce can apricot halves, drained
2 tablespoons kirsch

Heat the dried apricots and orange juice in a heavy-bottomed saucepan over a medium heat, until the apricots are soft.

Puree the softened apricots, orange juice and orange rind in a blender or food processor until smooth. Add the canned apricots and kirsch and blend well. If the sauce is too thick, add more orange juice. The sauce can be served hot or cold; if served hot, reheat it in a double boiler.